MINORITY MEN IN A MAJORITY SETTING:

MIDDLE-LEVEL FRANCOPHONES IN THE CANADIAN PUBLIC SERVICE

MINORITY MEN IN A MAJORITY SETTING:
MIDDLE-LEVEL FRANCOPHONES IN THE CANADIAN PUBLIC SERVICE

Christopher Beattie

A Carleton Original
The Carleton Library No. 92
McClelland and Stewart Limited

THE CARLETON LIBRARY

A series of Canadian reprints, original works and new collections of source material relating to Canada, issued under the editorial supervision of the Institute of Canadian Studies of Carleton University, Ottawa.

Contents

To M. and M., my dear parents,
and to my Hudson in-laws

Preface

It will be immediately obvious to the reader of what follows that the findings on which this book is based could not have been gathered by one man alone. The book is indeed one of the by-products of the efforts of a research team. The team was in operation from 1965 to 1968 in order to carry out a study for the Canadian government's Royal Commission on Bilingualism and Biculturalism. In the early stages, George Torrance, Jacques Désy and I developed the interview schedule and sampling design. We received guidance from Oswald Hall of the University of Toronto, John W. C. Johnstone of the National Opinion Research Center, University of Chicago, and Marjorie N. Donald of Carleton University. Our understanding of the five departments selected for study was enhanced by Wes Bolstad of the University of Saskatchewan, Maureen Appel, and Peter Pitsiladis of Sir George Williams University. They examined the formal structure of these departments before the interviewing commenced and provided our interviewers with background information.

S.A. Longstaff joined the study soon after the interviewing began. Désy, Torrance, Longstaff, and I conducted many of the early interviews and began the analysis of the findings. However, the bulk of the interviews, the coding of responses, and many preliminary tabulations were done by a group of youthful researchers: Carol Morgan Angi, Anne Dixson, François Dorlot, Luc-Gilbert Lessard, Pierre Poirier, André Robert, Roma Standefer, Raymond Taillon, Martin Thériault, Barbara Milne Thompson, Barry Thompson, and Sharron Welsh.

Punching the data onto cards and processing the many requests for computations were chores ably done by S.M.A. Inc. (Société de Mathématiques Appliquées) of Montreal. I am grateful to Jean Fortier, Michel Mailloux, and their supporting staff. Byron G. Spencer, Department of Economics, McMaster University, provided me with invaluable aid in the execution and interpretation of the multiple-regression results reported in Chapter Four.

From the start of the research until its completion my research supervisor at the Royal Commission, Meyer Brownstone, now of the Department of Political Economy, University of Toronto, was a constant source of aid.

Some preliminary findings from this study have already been published: Christopher Beattie, Jacques Désy, and S.A. Longstaff, *Bureaucratic Careers: Anglophones and Francophones in the Canadian Public Service* (Ottawa, 1971). The present work goes into greater depth in fewer problem areas, is more concerned with theoretical issues in the field of majority-minority relations, and makes a greater effort at an explanatory synthesis than does the earlier book. My current approach reflects the influence of Professor Harold L. Wilensky, Department of Sociology, University of California, Berkeley. The book grew out of a doctoral thesis which I prepared under Professor Wilensky's guidance. He encouraged me to try to answer various theoretical questions with my data and applied his excellent editorial skills to my written answers. His own writings have provided a model of sociological analysis which I have tried to emulate.

Other California sociologists, Nathan Keyfitz, Department of Demography, University of California, Berkeley, and Ivan Vallier, Crown College, University of California, Santa Cruz, each made important contributions to the unfolding of the book. The article "Canadians and Canadiens" published by Professor Keyfitz in the *Queen's Quarterly* (1963) is still the most sensitive treatment available of the situation of Francophones in "English" organizations. I have tried to pursue further some of the ideas which he advances in that article. Having him available for personal consultation was of great assistance. I owe whatever sensitivity to the historical and comparative dimensions of the research problems which this thesis addresses to the encouragement of Professor Vallier. Neil Smelser and Arthur Stinchcombe have made me more aware of theoretical and methodological problems and their interrelatedness. Reinhard Bendix approved of a paper on elite groups in Canada which I wrote; this motivated me to further efforts in this area.

In Ottawa, Berkeley, and Toronto I received amiable and expert aid in the typing of drafts of my various chapters. Jacqueline Goyette and Andrée Traversy in Ottawa, Sharon

Richards in Berkeley, Beryl Merrick, Elaine Yates and Joyce O'Keefe in Toronto all worked beyond the call of duty.

Finally, I offer this small sentence as a meagre testament to the large debt I owe my editor, proofreader, constant source of inspiration, and wife, Judy.

Christopher Beattie
Toronto, 1974.

Chapter One

Introduction

The theme that societies or social organizations present two faces is a prominent one in the sociological literature. Within a social system there can be order but also conflict, stability but also change, integration but also structural separation.[1] One person can evaluate and treat another in both intimate and impersonal terms. Two men in a large organization may be linked by both formal and informal ties, and respond differently to each other according to which network is activated. Such "dual tendencies"[2] present the sociological imagination with challenging problems of description and explanation.

This report focuses on the interplay between forces of integration and separation: members of a modern society are tied to one another by bonds of various kinds so that they develop a national identity, but these same members also participate in "subsocieties" of varying strengths that are based on an ethnic-religious heritage, often reinforced by language. One can see the workings of this process by studying people of diverse ethnic-religious origins in large bureaucracies. Bureaucracies, and the careers they offer, draw people away from their local ties into the national mainstream. Such organizations bind together the people who depend on them for income. Thus bureaucratic organizations are sources of societal integration but they are composed of members of many subsocieties. The study of ethnic groups in bureaucracies provides insights into the dual tendencies of integration and separation. I will attempt to disentangle the ways that ties to ethnic, religious, and linguistic roots, and ties to differing organizations and careers combine to influence social conduct.[3] Or, more exactly, I will (1) explore the interplay between ethnic-religious and regional cultures on the one hand, and organizational and occupational cultures on the other hand, and (2) demonstrate the relative influence of ethnic-religious and regional origins, type of organization, and type of occupation as determinants of the types of men who seek out employment in these organizations, attitudes about work, rates of career advancement, and the process of assimilation of minority men, also taking into account such factors as age, seniority, and level and quality of education.

The specific groups under study are the subordinate "Francophones" and the dominant "Anglophones." This terminology, borrowed from the French language, indicates the "tuning in" and attachment to one or the other of the two major ethnic-linguistic cultures in Canada. Francophone and Anglophone are terms which apply to nearly all Canadians depending on whether they are oriented to and identify with the mass media, voluntary associations, economic units, or political affairs of either the French or the English Sector. In my samples, the Francophones turned out to be almost all of French ethnicity (97 per cent) and Roman Catholic religion (94 percent), while 73 per cent of the Anglophones were of the Protestant faith. Thus, members of the Francophone and Anglophone groups are from quite different ethnic, linguistic, and, in large measure, religious backgrounds.

The organizations under study are five very different departments of the Canadian federal administration. Each is quite autonomous and has developed its own distinctive culture or ethos; together they represent a wide range of formal structures and corporate functions. Five departments were chosen as a representative cross-section of the types of departmental structures and functions in the federal administration. The Department of Finance is one of the central, powerful, policy-advising agencies in the government. Its officers are responsible for the study and development of Canada's domestic and international financial policies. There are fewer than 100 officers (middle-level and above) manning the core of the department. The second department, the Department of Agriculture, is a dual-purpose organization. It contains a large staff of agricultural scientists doing basic research, as well as a service organization that safeguards the quality of produce put on the market and provides advice to the farming community. It is the seventh largest department among the twenty-three departments which make up the federal administration and has a staff of about 8,000 located across Canada. The Department of National Revenue, the third largest department of the government, is responsible for the collection of income and other taxes, as well as customs and excise charges through a network of regional offices. Like several other departments, it is called upon to deal directly with many tax-paying citizens. I studied only one of its two main divisions, the Taxation Division, which contained about 6,600 employees. The Department of Public Works is also a large one (8,800 persons) and is charged with the construction and maintenance of all federal buildings, roads, bridges, wharves and other properties. Like National Revenue (Taxation), it maintains a string of regional offices though these are not for dealing with the public, but rather to organize local operations. The last department studied, the Department of the Secretary of State, was composed of three quite autonomous sectors, each concerned with the protection or extension of Canadian culture: National Museum, Translation Bureau, and Patent Office. The units ranged in size from about 400 in the Patent Office and Translation Bureau to 165 in the National Museum, of which nearly all staff were located in the capital area.

Obviously these organizations differ markedly in corporate culture and occupational components. A wide variety of careerists is included: policy makers, research scientists, tax men, engineers and technical specialists, translators, patent engineers, and museum administrators and researchers. These diverse careerists can be placed in three categories, each containing persons with common career characteristics. *Professional and scientific* careers are based on the possession of specialized training at the university level. Respondents in both the sciences and the professions usually have a strong attachment to the discipline in which they received their training. In *technical and semi-professional* careers persons perform specialized tasks in an area related to one of the sciences or professions. Generally, they lack the university or other credentials that would permit them to obtain senior positions. Again, most of these persons, like the professionals and scientists, have specialist knowledge about a complex biological or engineering process. The *administrative* category encompasses the broad area of work in which the principal activity is the development of policy or the management of operations, or both. Careers in this field usually require skill in developing ideas or in handling men. Administrators are typically generalists with a non-specialist university education. The five departments and the career lines running through them provide a great variety of stages on which to view the play of forces of integration and separation.

Although my findings are drawn from a survey conducted among middle-level employees at mid-career in several Canadian organizations, I think that my conclusions can be used to generate hypotheses about the experiences of white employees at the middle level of an important class of complex organizations in the Anglo-American democracies (Britain, Canada, United States, Australia), specifically, organizations that employ persons of a variety of white ethnicities but are dominated by WASPs (White, Anglo-Saxon, Protestants) who also dominate the elites of the wider society. Following Wilensky and Ladinsky,[4] I will refer to these WASPs who dominate both the elites and many key organizations in the Anglo-American democracies as *majority men*, and the organizations they dominate as *majority settings*. Those of other origins who populate these organizations are *minority men*. This study, then, is an examination of majority-minority relations in majority settings.

For any analysis of the determinants of job fate, the distinction between majority and minority men is crucial. It is clear that majority men in majority settings rarely experience situations where their ethnic-religious culture is at odds with the cultures of organization or career, while minority men often do so. Moreover, minority men in such settings may find themselves singled out for discrimination simply because of their ethnic-religious origins. For it is a commonplace that persons at work are evaluated not only in terms of what they do and how they do it, but also in terms of aspects of their person irrelevant to work performance. Thus organizational procedures, both formal rules and informal practices, assist some types of persons in advancing farther and faster than other types who have similar qualifications. Furthermore, the fact that men of different origins proceed at different rates up the career ladders in bureaucracies can result in prospective candidates learning what happens to people like themselves in these organizations and what they learn greatly influences their attitude toward employment in the units. Minority men who do decide to start off on a career are likely to possess quite different qualifications than majority men and reveal quite different career motives.

These considerations raise a host of research questions and suggest relevant hypotheses.

Question 1.   How do majority and minority men differ in terms of social background, education, and work history, and do these factors affect entry to a bureaucratic career?

Hypothesis 1:   Minority men are drawn from a narrower geographic area, lower social origins, with less education and little other work experience.

Question 2.   Does taking a job in a majority setting have different meanings for majority and minority men?

Hypothesis 2:   Minority men are more prone to seek security and economic benefits in work where majority men are more motivated by the intrinsic interest of the job itself.

Question 3.   Are there differences in salary attainment and rate of career mobility for majority and minority men with similar qualifications?

Hypothesis 3:   Majority men will have a significant salary advantage over their minority equivalents and will have a higher rate of career mobility.

Question 4.   In what types of organizations and careers do minority men maintain the most viable ties to their ethnic-religious roots? Does employment in a majority setting mean the inevitable abandonment of the ethnic community off the job?

Hypothesis 4:   Minority men in routine work areas are able to maintain viable ties to their ethnic-religious roots.

In testing these hypotheses it was important to separate out and weigh the relative influences of ethnic-religious culture, class background, regional culture, and organizational or career cultures. A sample was selected and an interview schedule developed to permit me to do this. I concentrated on persons who had reached a point where they had several years of their work-life behind them, either outside or inside government service, and now faced the prospect of a lifetime career in the federal administration. These middle-level men were senior but young men who expected the future to be one of advancement.

To insure that only persons of officer status were included, everyone making less than sixty-two hundred dollars ($6,200) a year (1965) was eliminated. No upper limit on salary was set. This meant that I would corral only those who had professional or technical expertise, or a responsible administrative post. In short, I wanted to get those who represented the dominant ethos of their department. They might wield substantial power, though most usually do not, but most have a chance to become important men. Some will eventually make it to the elite.

A second consideration involved the stage of the career. On the one hand I avoided those not likely to be settled on a career choice by setting a lower age-limit of 25. On the other hand, I sought to exclude those who had reached the upper limits of their capacities, those who had settled into bureaucratic ruts, and those generally too old to receive major promotions. I chose an upper age limit of forty-five to eliminate many such men.

I wanted to tap the full details of the respondent's educational and work history, and cover, as well, his attitudes about his present job and work organization. A personal interview was in order. It involved standardized questions for all respondents. Many of the questions contained suggested "probes" that the interviewer could use as a follow-up to the original question in order to gain more detail from the respondent. Some of the question items contained in the interview schedule were developed in French; most originated in English. The translation was done by members of the research team. After pretesting, a number of questions were dropped or reformulated and a final version of the interview developed.

The French and English versions are the same save in areas covering language ability and usage. Here the Anglophones were asked questions about the amount of ability they felt they had in the French language and the degree to which they used or thought they could use French in their work. The Francophone respondents were asked similar questions about their capacity in and use of English.

The interview began with a review of the respondent's education and work experience outside the federal administration. It then went on to cover his reasons for joining the public service and various posts held in the course of his work with the government. A number of questions dwelt on attitudes and perceptions about the federal service as a work-place. Here, the person was asked about the ways and means to success in the civil service. There was a section on language usage and contacts with members of the other language group. Another section covered attitudes toward the recent emphasis on bilingualism in the public service. The interview finished with a series of questions on how the public servant viewed the Ottawa-Hull region as a place to live and work.

After completion of the interview, the respondents were handed a short questionnaire to fill in. It elicited additional information about the respondent's birthplace, father, marital status, religious and other associational memberships, second language skills, and several other topics.[5]

The original plan was to draw a random sample of 30-35 Francophones and 30-35 Anglophones from lists provided by each department of persons in our age and salary brackets. When the lists arrived it became clear that the plan would have to be modified. When the population was divided into Francophone and Anglophone segments, the number of Francophones in four of the five departments precluded the possibility of sampling.[6] In these four departments all the Francophones were interviewed. However, among the Anglophones in all five departments and in one department—Secretary of State—where large numbers of Francophones were located, random sampling was used. Table 1.1 shows the size of the Francophone and Anglophone population falling within the established age and salary boundaries in each department, and, where necessary, the random sample selected from it for interviewing. Only one man refused to be interviewed; he was employed in the Department of Public Works. Thus, I had a final total of 168 interviews with Anglophones and 128 with Francophones.

When these interviews with middle-level men between 25 and 45 years of age working in five government bureaucracies were completed, I had available 296 life stories. The story of each man began with his early involvements in an ethnic-religious heritage, linguistic tradition, and regional milieu. It carried on into his educational experiences and first steps along a career route. Then it followed him through the work world to the government department which employed him at the time of

TABLE 1.1

Ethnic-Linguistic Composition of the Population of Canadian Public Servants in the National Capital Area Between 25 and 45 Years of Age Earning $6,200 or More Per Annum in 1965 and Those Chosen for Interviewing by Selected Departments

Selected Department	Anglophones		Francophones		Total Population
	Population	Chosen for Interview	Population	Inter-view	
Finance	48	28	6	6	54
Agriculture	279	37	28	28	307
National Revenue (Taxation)	154	33	33	33	187
Public Works	173	32 (33)	28	28	201
Secretary of State	114	38	57	33	171
TOTAL	768	168 (169)	152	128	920

the study. Thus three aspects of each man's life are in focus: early socialization, career type, organizational setting. This structure helped me assess the ways in which an identity acquired early in life affects career choices and success and commitment to an organization and its mission.

The fact that lives of Anglophones, a dominant group, are compared to lives of Francophones, a subordinate group, adds both specificity and generality. The findings reveal some specifics of intergroup relations in Canada. Beyond this, if Francophones, carriers of a legitimate and "official" culture, find that career and organizational cultures produce an erosion of their ethnic and religious culture and that their very ethnic-religious identity brings them unequal treatment, then other white minorities must surely be under greater pressure to assimilate and face even greater inequities. The special status of Francophones in Canada ought to reduce or deflect integrative pressures brought to bear on them. If this study finds that the Francophone minority are culturally overwhelmed by an Anglophone majority and that the majority group systematically slows the career mobility of minority men, it can be asserted that other white minorities in Anglo-American societies are likely subject to the same processes with even greater effects.

Notes

[1] The goal of explaining both order and conflict within the corpus of a single body of sociological theory has occasioned the most debate. It concerns, specifically, the capacity of "structural-functional" theory as exemplified in the writings of Talcott Parsons to explain the genesis of conflict and structural change. There are many contributors to the debate and the issues are rather hard to summarize easily but an overview is provided by N. J. Demerath III and Richard A. Peterson (eds.), *System, Change, and Conflict, A Reader on Contemporary Functional Theory and the Debate Over Functionalism* (New York, 1967).

[2] Reinhard Bendix and Bennett Berger, "Images of Society and Problems of Concept Formation in Sociology" in Llewellyn Gross (ed.), *Symposium on Sociological Theory* (Evanston, Ill., 1959), pp. 92-118.

[3] This formulation of the problem borrows much from Harold L. Wilensky, "Work, Careers, and Social Integration," *International Social Science Journal*, 12 (Fall, 1960), pp. 543-60.

[4] Harold L. Wilensky and Jack Ladinsky, "From Religious Community to Occupational Group: Structural Assimilation Among Professors, Lawyers, and Engineers," *American Sociological Review*, 32 (August, 1967), pp. 541-61.

[5] The complete English and French versions of both interview and questionnaire are provided as Appendix IV. Beattie, *et al.*

[6] In accordance with our distinction between Anglophones and Francophones we began by checking the departmental lists for those with French names, and, on some lists, French mother tongue. Then a check was made with departmental officials to determine if any person who did not speak French and did not consider himself "French" had been included. As well, we asked if any person who regarded himself as a French Canadian and was fluent in the French tongue had been missed. Even with this checking, however, we found one or two assumed Francophones who, when contact was made by phone to set up an interview, professed limited ability in French and identified completely with English-speaking Canada. These persons were shifted into the relevant Anglophone population and became eligible for selection in the Anglophone sample.

Chapter Two

The Backgrounds of Middle-Level Men

It is the elite level of a nation's public service that most often catches the attention of the social researcher. Australia, Britain, Egypt, Germany, India, Japan, Pakistan, and the United States are among those countries that have had a collective portrait drawn of their higher public servants.[1] Canada is also a member of this club. John Porter has contributed a study of the composition of the "bureaucratic elite" as of 1953.[2]

Researchers rarely focus on the primary recruiting ground of the bureaucratic elite: middle-level men at mid-career. The mechanisms of career advancement that move men through the middle-level and propel some into the elite have not been uncovered. To obtain some idea about the types of men who move faster and farther through the middle rank, this chapter will compare the composition of elite and middle levels. By examining those who have "made it" into the elite, we can derive some hunches as to who is likely to have a meteoric career at the middle level.

A. The Bureaucratic Elite

Porter located 207 members of the elite in 1953—41 at the deputy minister level, 89 at the assistant- or associate-deputy level, and 77 at the director level, or the equivalent.[3] He added to this group an additional 36 senior executives of Crown Corporations although he recognizes that they are out of the mainstream of the Public Service.[4] No doubt the numbers in elite positions have increased greatly from the 243 in 1953.

Porter's theme is not the size of the elite, rather its homogeneity. His findings are given further support in the careful journalism of Peter C. Newman.[5] Newman's gaze, however, is directed only to the most powerful segment of the elite—specifically to 18 acting civil servants and 12 "alumni" who in 1964 constituted the inner circle of the "Ottawa Establishment." Both the Porter and Newman portrayals stress the following: recruitment from middle- and upper-class backgrounds; the prevalence of university degrees and especially graduate work in economics, politics, or history, frequently in Britain; and a strong possibility of university teaching either somewhere in the past or projected for the future. There is an orientation toward intellectual values and relative isolation from worlds other than the university or Ottawa political community.

The intellectualism of the elite has been commented on in another context. Several writers have noted that the upper reaches of the Public Service are more comfortable working for Liberal governments than they are under the more doctrinaire Conservatives.[6] John Meisel even indicates that public servants, not party officials, were the creative source of the Liberal programme in the general election of 1957.[7]

The homogeneity of the elite pictured by Porter and the others stands in contrast to the diversity of the middle level which I uncover in my sample.

B. Birthplace and Geographic Origins

The middle level of the federal administration contains a substantial proportion of "New Canadians," persons born abroad who represent a "brain gain" for Canada. In this, it resembles the labour force as a whole. In both the total labour force and the managerial, professional-technical labour force, slightly more than a fifth of the persons were born outside Canada (Figure 2.1). At the middle-level of the Public Service, about 22 per cent were born abroad.[8] Those born in the United Kingdom make the largest contribution. Fully 9 per cent of all middle-level public servants were born in that country.

A different picture emerges when one compares Anglophone and Francophone public servants at the middle level. Ninety-three per cent of the Francophones were born in Canada, but only 74 per cent of the Anglophones. Nearly 11 per cent of the Anglophones were born in the United Kingdom and 15 per cent come from other foreign countries. It is apparent, then, that while the Anglophone group contains a sizeable contingent of persons born abroad, such an extensive influx of new talent does not exist for the Francophones.

Of the persons born within Canada, nine out of ten of the Francophones are from either Ontario or Quebec (Table 2.1). To be exact, 51 per cent of the Francophone middle-level is from Quebec and 40 per cent from Ontario. This represents a decided overrepresentation of Franco-Ontarians since less than 10 per cent of the total French Canadian population resides there. The Anglophone group at the middle-level, on the other hand, contains a large corps (32%) from Western Canada. But, like the Francophones, the central provinces of Ontario and Quebec contribute a majority of the Anglophones. However, unlike the Francophones, only 6 per cent were born in Quebec but 49 per cent in Ontario. The Quebec figure is not exceedingly low if it is considered that only 6-7 per cent of Canadians of English mother tongue live in Quebec. There are relatively more Anglophones than Francophones drawn from the Atlantic Provinces but in both groups the proportion is quite small.

A relevant comparison to make is between the regional origins of the public servants and the distribution of the general population. Porter, for instance, finds that only one region —Ontario—is over-represented in the bureaucratic elite.[9] While the Prairie Provinces are close to proportional representation, British Columbia, the Atlantic Provinces and Quebec are under-represented. Quebec is the most under-represented of all. Considering my findings and the 1961 Census, a slightly different pattern emerges. Only one province—Quebec—is under-represented; but again, Ontario is the only province over-represented. Ontario is solidly over-represented with 34 per cent of the 1961 population but 49 per cent of the middle-level personnel. The Atlantic Provinces and Western Canada approach parity. The Atlantic Provinces have 10.4 per cent of the population and 10.5 per cent of the public servants; the Western provinces (British Columbia is included here also) share about 26 per cent of both the general population and the middle level. Quebec, again, is solidly under-represented. It holds 29 per cent of the Canadian population but only 15 per cent of the public servants come from there. Porter's comments about this situation in the elite would also seem to apply to the middle level: "The under-representation of Quebec can be considered an ethnic and educational factor rather than a regional one."[10]

It is commonplace that the highly trained and talented in industrial societies are likely to be mobile and that large-scale economic organizations, both public and private, encourage such movement. A mobile labour force is conducive to economic growth, permitting both easy expansion in one part of the country and the curtailment of production in another. Of course, it is also true that geographical mobility has its costs, especially in terms of the disruption or even severing of ties with family and friends, and the difficulties of adjusting to strange environments.

With the widespread geographical mobility of the Canadian population, persons may easily be born in one locality, yet come to maturity and perhaps form early attachments to another. It was decided, therefore, that the most meaningful way to determine the geographical origins of public servants would be to consider place of family residence during the years of secondary education. Data of this kind on middle-level personnel now working in the Ottawa and Hull area indicate a sharp contrast between Anglophones and Francophones (Table 2.2). Among Anglophones 19 per cent grew up in Ottawa-Hull; 52 per cent originated from points outside the provinces of Ontario and Quebec, including 21 per cent from foreign countries. Among Francophones what is noteworthy is the high proportion (43 per cent) from Ottawa and Hull. The narrow base of Francophone recruitment is even more striking when the numbers from the proximate French-speaking areas of Ontario are added to it, bringing the total to 51 per cent. In contrast, only 37 per cent originated from Montreal or other points in Quebec (excepting Hull). These data suggest that the federal administration has a good deal of success in recruiting Anglophones from all over Canada and even from around the world for work in the Capital, but the Francophones located in the middle reaches of government service are to a large extent natives of the Capital Region or its immediate environs.

It is noteworthy that the Capital Region serves as a greater source of Francophone talent for those departments like Public Works (61 per cent from Ottawa and Hull) and National

FIGURE 2.1

Place of Birth of Francophones and Anglophones at the Middle Level of the Canadian Public Service (1965) and of the Total Managerial and Professional-Technical Labour Force (1961) and Total Labour Force (1961) in Canada

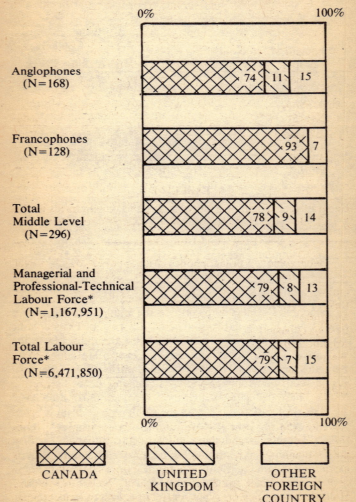

* *Census of Canada, 1961*, Volume III, Part 1.

TABLE 2.1

Place of Birth of Francophones and Anglophones Born in Canada and Now Working at the Middle Level of the Canadian Public Service (1965)

Linguistic Group	Place of Birth				
	Atlantic Provinces	Quebec	Ontario	Western Canada	Total
Francophones (N:119)	5	51	40	4	100
Anglophones (N:125)	12	6	50	31	99
Total Middle Level (N:244)	11	15	49	26	101

TABLE 2.2

Geographical Origin of Francophones and Anglophones at the Middle Level of the Canadian Public Service (1965)

Geographic Origin	Francophones (N:128)	Anglophones (N:168)	Total Middle Level (N:296)
Ottawa and Hull	43%	19%	22%
Rest of Ontario	8	23	21
Montreal	13	4	6
Rest of Quebec	23	2	5
Atlantic Provinces	4	8	8
Western Canada	3	23	20
Foreign Country	6	21	18
Total	100%	100%	100%

Revenue (58 per cent), where routine "housekeeping" functions predominate and there are few possibilities for either policy-planning or research. By contrast Agriculture, which carries out important scientific activities, draws half of its Francophone personnel from the province of Quebec (excluding Hull). In terms of career types, only 21 per cent of Francophone professionals and scientists come from Ottawa and Hull, but 65

of francophones or
from PQ or
from Ontario

16   MINORITY MEN IN A MAJORITY SETTING

per cent of the administrators and 48 per cent of technical and semi-professionals do. It is clear that the Capital Region provides few skilled Francophone scientists and professionals for government work. Such persons must be attracted from the Province of Quebec.

Here is the first "hard" evidence of the polarity in the Francophone group between *Québecois* and Franco-Ontarians. The *Québecois* were raised in the heartland of French Canada and had access to a complete system of French-language schools. By contrast, the Franco-Ontarians or, for that matter, any Francophones raised outside the Province of Quebec, were unable to obtain a complete education in French. As we shall see, young Francophones subjected to an English education become school dropouts at an extremely high rate. The upshot is that *Québecois* tend to receive educations that are much more substantial than those of the Franco-Ontarians.

There are many more grounds on which *Québecois* and Franco-Ontarians differ. In the following pages other fundamental distinctions between the two will be identified and linked.

The Anglophone professionals and scientists, like their Francophone counterparts, draw few (8 per cent) of their numbers from the Capital area. On the other hand, 26 per cent of the administrators and 29 per cent of the technical and semi-professionals come from here. The rest of Ontario, apart from Ottawa, is an important source of specialists. A fifth of the professional and scientists and 31 per cent of the technical and semi-professional personnel spent their teenage years here.

Western Canada is the place of origin for a large corps of Anglophones in certain departments and careers. Except for Public Works, a quarter or more in each department studied is from one of the Western provinces. Administrators more than the other two career types are drawn from here. Nearly four in ten of them (38 per cent) are from Western Canada compared to 23 per cent and 17 per cent among the professionals and scientists, and technicians and semi-professionals, respectively. Of note is that one type of administrator—the Finance Officer —draws 44 per cent of his numbers from the West.

With regard to those who grew up in foreign countries, they are disproportionately likely to be pursuing scientific and professional careers. In fact 29 per cent of those in the Anglophone sample and an estimated 25 per cent of the total sample pursuing professional-scientific careers are of foreign origin. This lends strong support to a point made by John Porter: because of the inadequacy of the professional, scientific, and technical training in Canada, she must rely heavily on graduates from other countries.[11] In this respect Canada is doubly fortunate. Not only does she reap the benefits of these highly-trained immigrants, but she also manages to avoid the costly burden of educating them.

C. Ethnic and Religious Background

Earlier I indicated that although the Francophone group was nearly completely of French origin, the Anglophone group contained an infusion of non-British elements. When the two groups are combined and properly weighted to give a result for the total middle-level, it appears that 61 per cent is of British origin, 18 per cent of French, and 21 of other origins. These figures clearly indicate that those of French descent are under-represented at the middle level, whether one takes the managerial-professional or total labour force as a standard (Figure 2.2). It is clear also that the middle level is more British-dominated than the managerial-professional-technical labour force of the country. The latter, however, is more British-dominated than the total Canadian labour force.

The non-British, non-French element is certainly more prominent at the middle level than in the elite. Here John Porter tells us: "Other ethnic groups in Canada with the exception of Jews, are scarcely represented at all in the higher bureaucracy."[12] At the middle-level not only Jews but a variety of other ethnicities are present. While 3 per cent are Jewish, 10 per cent are of Northwestern European origins, and 6 per cent of Middle European or Slavic origins.

As with ethnicity, in religious memberships the Francophones reveal homogeneity and the Anglophones heterogeneity (Table 2.3). Ninety-four per cent of Francophones claim adherence to the Roman Catholic faith. On the Anglophone side, six out of ten belong to one of the Protestant

FIGURE 2.2

Ethnic Descent of Francophones and Anglophones at the Middle Level of the Canadian Public Service (1965) and of the Managerial and Professional-Technical Labour Force (1961) and the Total Labour Force (1961) in Canada

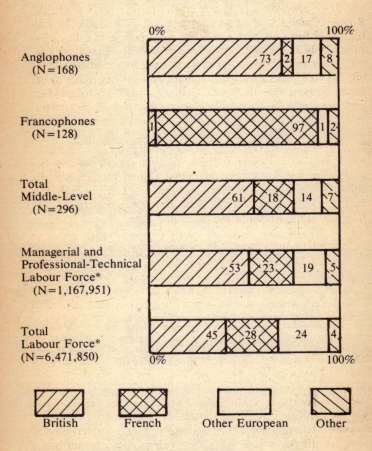

* *Census of Canada, 1961*, Volume 3, Part 1.

religions, but nearly a quarter are Roman Catholic. Interestingly, 9 per cent of the Anglophones declare they are either agnostics or atheists. Only one person among the Francophones (0.8 per cent) made such a declaration.

Compared to the total Canadian population, the Protestants and Jews are over-represented at the middle level while the Roman Catholics are under-represented. While the Roman Catholics form 46 per cent of the total population they contribute only 36 per cent to the segment of the federal administration under study. However, as we will see in a moment, this is not due to a general lack of Roman Catholics but rather to the absence of one specific type of Catholic—the French Catholic.

A comparison of the religious membership of the bureaucratic elite and the middle level is hampered by the fact that Porter lacked information about religious affiliation for 35 per cent of the elite.[13] The data on the remainder show 23 per cent belonging to the Roman Catholic Church and 67 per cent belonging to various Protestant faiths: United Church (29 per cent), Anglican (23 per cent), Presbyterian (10 per cent) and Baptist (5 per cent). Porter compares these findings to the religious composition of the economic elite.

First, the nonconformist Protestant denominations replaced Anglicanism as the dominant faiths, and, secondly, the Roman Catholic church had a greater proportion of adherents in the bureaucratic than in the economic elite although it was still very much under-represented when compared to the Catholic proportion of the general population.[14]

I would add that the middle level contains a smaller proportion of Protestants and a larger proportion of Roman Catholics than the elite; proportions which more nearly reflect the distribution of religious membership in the Canadian population. Thus, the middle level shows greater religious variety than the elite; it is not as dominated by Protestantism.

I would disagree with the emphasis of Porter's assertion that the Catholic under-representation "can probably be attributed to inadequate educational facilities and the lower social class base of Catholicism."[15] More importantly, Catholic under-representation in the Public Service is accounted for by the lack

TABLE 2.3

Religious Membership Among Francophones and Anglophones
at the Middle Level of the Canadian Public Service (1965) and
Among the Total Canadian Population (1961)

Linguistic Group	Religious Membership				
	Roman Catholic	Protestant	Jewish	Other or Not Determined	Total
Francophones (N:128)	94	2	1	4	101
Anglophones (N:168)	24	60	3	13	100
Total Middle Level (N:296)	36	50	3	12	101
Total Canadian Population* (N:18,238,249)	46	41	1	12	100

* *Census of Canada,* 1961, Volume I, Part 2.

of French Canadians who by and large are also Roman
Catholics. In fact, a rough comparison between the proportion
of middle-level Anglophones who are Roman Catholic and the
proportion of Catholics in the total Anglophone population of
Canada (i.e., the non-French Canadian) shows no difference. In
other words, Anglophone Catholics are adequately represented
in the Public Service; it is the lack of Francophone Catholics that
accounts for the overall under-representation of the Roman
Catholic faith in the federal administration. The important thing
is not that Catholics in general lack adequate educational
facilities and come from low social origins—although this may
be true—but rather that Francophone Catholics, for reasons that
would include educational and class factors among others, have
a considerably lower rate of participation in the Public Service.

D. Rural-Urban and Social Class Background

In the "Introduction" I discussed how the large groupings

which provide a pluralistic base for a society tend to be rooted in a particular region, a rural or urban culture, and tend to be concentrated at a certain class level. Among the Francophones we have already begun to see the presence of two regional subsocieties: *Québecois* and Franco-Ontarians. The Anglophones reveal greater diversity in regional cultures.

Now I report on the rural or urban character of the place where the middle-level men spent their teenage years. The places were categorized according to their size in 1941, a year in which many of the respondents would have been in their teens.

It appears that the Anglophone officers were more likely than the Francophones to live in large cities during their teenage years. Eighteen per cent of the Francophones but 27 per cent of the Anglophones are from cities of over 250,000 population (in 1941) (Table 2.4). However, more than half the Francophones were raised in medium-sized cities (50,000-250,000) but only a third of the Anglophones. The high figure for Francophones is largely accounted for by heavy government recruitment from the local Ottawa and Hull area. Thus, the Francophones are more "urbanized" than the Anglophones, if we take urban to mean growing up in either a large or medium-sized city. Seven in ten of the Francophones are from such settings compared to six in ten of the Anglophones. About 14 to 15 per cent of both language groups spent their early days in a small village or a rural area.

These findings reveal that the majority of public servants at the middle level are bearers of an urban culture. I suspect that even those from rural or small-town origins have been quite immersed in an urban ambiance. It would seem that specific features of rural culture have meagre meaning for them now and affect their behaviour but little. For the time being, however, I will leave open the question of the urban character of public servants.

A social class is, at base, rooted in objective but changeable differences between persons. The most important differences are economic. A social class is a stratum consisting of families or individuals who share a common economic position as indicated by occupation, wealth or the ownership of property; the stratum is higher or lower than one or more other strata. Also, the differences are changeable in that social classes, unlike

TABLE 2.4

Size of Place of Origin (as of 1941) of Francophones and Anglophones at the Middle Level of the Canadian Public Service (1965)

	Size of Place of Origin						
Linguistic Group	Large City (250,000 or more)	Medium City (50,000- 250,000)	Small City (10,000- 50,000)	Towns (2,500- 10,000)	Village or Rural	Not deter- mined	Total
Francophones (N:128)	18	53	13	2	14	0	100
Anglophones (N:168)	26	32	14	10	13	5	100
Total Middle Level (N:296)	25	36	14	9	13	4	101

castes which are entered and fixed at birth, are relatively "open." A person or family can move up or down in class levels in the course of a generation. In the first instance, then, social classes are rooted in economic differences between persons. But economic differences become the basis of subjective awareness. Those in a social class share a definite "style of life," are more likely to mix with others who share the same life-style, and develop a sense of who is like themselves, who superior and who inferior. Whether or not class becomes subjectively experienced, the economic differences on which it rests affect a wide range of behaviour and attitudes. Certain lines of action are more likely to be available or blocked, and certain beliefs either affirmed or denied, depending on class position. It is this aspect of social class which is of interest here. I ask: does class origin have a significant bearing on gaining entry to the federal Public Service?

In the present analysis, social class background is measured by the occupation, income, and education of the respondent's father.[16] Upper or upper-middle class origin includes those whose fathers were in managerial or professional occupations, usually possessed a university degree, and received a high salary. The lower-middle class encompasses persons with fathers in "white-collar" work of a non-professional variety (i.e., sales, clerking, low-level administration). Typically, these fathers have some secondary school education and may even have completed high school, but they have not attended university. A working class background includes those with fathers who were skilled tradesmen, semi-skilled tradesmen, or industrial labourers. A farm background includes the civil servants whose fathers were either farm owners or farm labourers. The distribution of Francophones and Anglophones among these four classes is shown in Figure 2.3.

FIGURE 2.3

Social Class Background of Francophones and Anglophones at the Middle Level of the Canadian Public Service (1965)

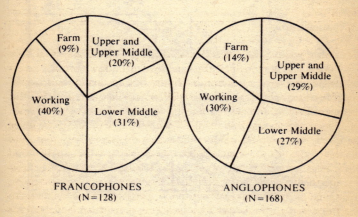

FRANCOPHONES
(N=128)

ANGLOPHONES
(N=168)

The Anglophone group contains a relatively higher proportion of persons of upper and upper-middle class backgrounds than does the Francophone group. Especially noteworthy, however, is the functioning of the Public Service as an avenue of upward mobility for many Canadians of both linguistic communities. It offers respectable "white-collar" positions to persons from farming or working class backgrounds: 49 per cent of the Francophones and 44 per cent of the Anglophones. Although these proportions are sizeable, we will see in a moment

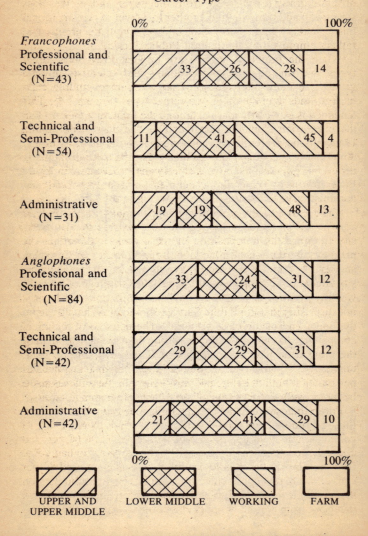

FIGURE 2.4

Social Class Background of Francophones and Anglophones at the Middle Level of the Canadian Public Service (1965) by Career Type

Francophones
Professional and Scientific (N=43): 33 | 26 | 28 | 14

Technical and Semi-Professional (N=54): 11 | 41 | 45 | 4

Administrative (N=31): 19 | 19 | 48 | 13

Anglophones
Professional and Scientific (N=84): 33 | 24 | 31 | 12

Technical and Semi-Professional (N=42): 29 | 29 | 31 | 12

Administrative (N=42): 21 | 41 | 29 | 10

UPPER AND UPPER MIDDLE   LOWER MIDDLE   WORKING   FARM

that they still reflect an unequal distribution of offices among the social classes. The figures do indicate, however, that the middle level is clearly not the sole preserve of a privileged collection of officials drawn exclusively from the upper end of the class system. In addition, we find a rather low level of organizational inheritance. About 15 per cent of both linguistic groups had fathers employed by the federal Public Service.

When the linguistic groups are broken down into career types, we find that the professionals and scientists in both groups are more likely to be of upper or upper-middle class backgrounds than the other two career types (Figure 2.4). This tendency is especially marked among the Francophones. In fact the proportion from the upper end of the class scale among Francophone professionals and scientists is as great as in any Anglophone category. This indicates that the overall linguistic difference pointed out above is chiefly to be accounted for by the lower origins of Francophone technical, semi-professional, and administrative employees.

Since entry to the middle and upper ranks of the federal administration increasingly requires the possession of university training, the composition of these ranks will reflect the unequal distribution of educational opportunities in Canadian society. As Porter and others[17] have shown, given that a university education in Canada is still largely the privilege of a small, wealthy group at or near the top of the occupational scale, it is not surprising that the Public Service should draw heavily from the upper end of the class system. "The demand of technical competence has narrowed the recruiting base to that fragment of the population who are willing and financially able to go to university."[18] However, despite a similar reliance on educated personnel at both the elite and middle levels, the elite seems to be more exclusive in terms of the educated persons it admits.

Porter indicates that the bureaucratic elite draws heavily from those of middle-class origins or higher. He finds that in 1953, 18 per cent came from upper class backgrounds while 69 per cent could be considered middle class.[19] Thus those who had come from families in the middle or higher classes composed 87 per cent of the bureaucratic elite. By contrast, background data on the middle level of the Public Service indicate that less than six in ten are from middle or upper class origins. Even if the criteria used to identify the middle or higher classes differ slightly between the two studies—and they do not appear to do so—this is still a striking difference indicative of the greater openness of the middle level.

Even so, while those of working class or farming origins constitute 45 per cent of the middle level, they probably make up about 60 per cent of the Canadian labour force (i.e., those in Blue Collar, Primary, Transportation, and Service occupations). Thus, while the middle level does not reflect the class distribution of the Canadian labour force it is certainly more open to persons from lower strata than is the elite. The Anglophone and Francophone groups at the middle level contain sizeable contingents of persons from both middle and working class origins.

It is now possible to see how the two ethnic-linguistic cultures of Anglophones and Francophones are subdivided into regional, class, and perhaps rural-urban components. The Francophone group, uniform in ethnicity and Roman Catholicism, contains two clear regional cultures, each regional culture divided in turn into middle and working class. The Anglophone group, with British and non-British, Protestant and Catholic segments, also contains several regional cultures, each stratified by class. And, to complicate matters further, each ethnic-religious-regional-class segment can be further divided into a rural or urban part. Not all these combinations will appear in what follows. Small numbers make it impossible to generalize about any more than a few of the combinations. However, I will be careful to identify the relative and separate strengths of ethnic-linguistic, religious, regional, class, and sometimes, rural-urban cultures on behaviour.

E. Education

With its emphasis on objective criteria for selecting and promoting its personnel, the Public Service makes much of education and training qualifications. In the future such qualifications will receive even more stress. As departments expand or take on new tasks and as organizational planning and rationality increase, educational qualifications, as against seniority, "practical" experience, or simple favouritism, will become even more crucial in determining an individual's fate.

The upper levels of the federal Public Service, according to Porter, contain "what is probably the most highly trained group of people to be found anywhere in Canada."[20] Among the 202 elite members (out of 243) for whom information was available, 79 per cent had university degrees; of those with degrees, 55 per cent had a higher degree (a degree beyond the "bachelors" or first degree level).[21] Also, nearly one in five (18 per cent) had taught in a university at some point in his or her worklife. Thus, the higher bureaucracy has about it the atmosphere of academe. "A medal from a learned society, an important article, a brief on some important economic, social, or scientific question enhances the individual's reputation within the system. In the departmental committee and at the less formal luncheon or social evening where ideas are put into circulation by some and evaluated by others, individuals become assessed on their intellectual abilities."[22] This commitment to education and intellectual pursuits is a distinctive feature of the bureaucratic elite.

It is not surprising that although the level of education at the middle level is high, it is not as high as in the elite. Overall, about 71 per cent have university degrees compared to 79 per cent in the elite. And this comparison favours the middle level since it is more than 10 years before my study was made (1953) that the data on the senior levels were obtained. We can assume that the level of education in the elite has risen in the interim, so the gap is probably wider than these figures suggest.

One gauge of the high level of education at the middle-level is to compare it with the managerial and professional-technical labour force. Here, 20 per cent possess university degrees. As we have seen, the university fraction is more than three times greater in the middle stratum of the Public Service.

There is a difference in level of education between the two linguistic groups at the middle level (Figure 2.5). The Francophone group contains relatively fewer persons with university degrees. Sixty-four per cent of the Francophones but 72 per cent of the Anglophones possess such degrees.

It is easier for persons without a university degree to reach the middle level in the large service-oriented departments (National Revenue, Public Works) than in the others. Two-thirds (67 per cent) of the Anglophones and over half (52 per cent) of the Francophones in National Revenue lack university degrees; in Public Works, 31 per cent of the Anglophones and 43 per cent of the Francophones. Non-degree holders are considerably less prominent in other departments. Among the Anglophones in Finance and State, 10 per cent or fewer are without degrees. In the Department of Agriculture 16 per cent of Anglophones and 18 per cent of Francophones lack university credentials. It is clear, then, that certain departments—those charged with policy, research, or engineering tasks—have a markedly higher level of education than those in which routine administration predominates.

When the linguistic groups are divided into career types it is obvious that the professionals and scientists have the highest level of training (Figure 2.6). On the other hand, a majority of the technical and semi-professional personnel in both linguistic groups lack university degrees.

Perhaps the most arresting finding concerns the difference in level of education between natives of the Ottawa-Hull area and those from elsewhere (Table 2.5). The majority of Francophones from the Capital Region have not obtained a university degree. This is largely the outcome of two processes: the high dropout rate of Francophones from the primary and secondary school systems in the Ottawa-Hull area (to be discussed at greater length in a moment) and their easier access to government jobs not requiring a university degree. Francophones in the Ottawa-Hull area have a comparative advantage over their brethren from further afield in hearing about federal positions for which a university degree is not a prerequisite. Such positions are rarely advertised in centres distant from the Capital. Those in the local area are much more likely than others to become aware of them. The main recruiting in Quebec is for degree-holders. So, it is not surprising that among those from the province of Quebec, eight out of ten possess degrees. But it should also be mentioned that Francophones who grow up in Quebec have readier access and easier adjustment to local educational institutions than do the Franco-Ontarians.

On the Anglophone side we also find a high proportion of persons lacking university degrees among those who grew up in the Capital. Obviously, knowledge about and access to posts

FIGURE 2.5

Level of Education of Francophones and Anglophones at the Middle Level of the Canadian Public Service (1965)

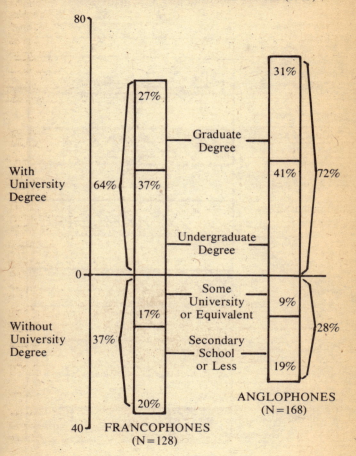

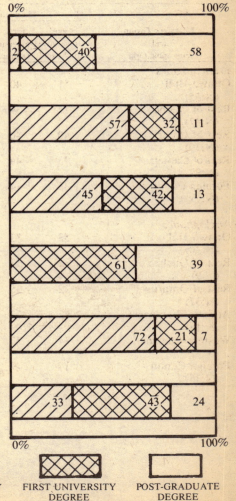

FIGURE 2.6

Level of Education of Francophones and Anglophones at the Middle Level of the Canadian Public Service (1965) by Career Type

Francophones
Professional and Scientific (N=43): 2, 40, 58

Technical and Semi-Professional (N=54): 57, 32, 11

Administrative (N=31): 45, 42, 13

Anglophones
Professional and Scientific (N=84): 61, 39

Technical and Semi-Professional (N=42): 72, 21, 7

Administrative (N=42): 33, 43, 24

NO UNIVERSITY DEGREE   FIRST UNIVERSITY DEGREE   POST-GRADUATE DEGREE

TABLE 2.5

Level of Education Among Francophones and Anglophones at the Middle Level of the Canadian Public Service (1965) by Geographic Origin

Linguistic Group and Geographic Origin	Level of Education			
	Some University or Less	First University Degree	Post-graduate Degree	% Total
Francophones				
Ottawa-Hull (N:55)	51	40	9	100
Rest of Quebec (N:47)	17	34	49	100
Rest of Ontario (N:10)	40	40	20	100
Rest of Canada (N:9)	33	44	22	99
Foreign Country (N:7)	43	14	43	100
Anglophones				
Ottawa-Hull (N:30)	53	33	13	99
Rest of Quebec (N:9)	33	33	33	99
Rest of Ontario (N:37)	32	35	32	99
Atlantic Provinces (N:15)	13	73	13	99
Western Canada (N:42)	14	57	29	100
Foreign Country (N:35)	14	49	37	100

where a university degree is not a prerequisite are greater for the local residents, both Anglophones and Francophones. Those Anglophones raised in areas distant from Ottawa contain in their ranks considerably larger proportions with university degrees.

Now I consider the types of educational routes which the two linguistic groups follow. Since the educational routes provided for Francophones and Anglophones are quite different, it can be expected that those who pass through them will emerge with differing aspirations and attitudes. Table 2.6 indicates the contrasts in educational experiences at the secondary school level.

TABLE 2.6

Type of Secondary School Attended by Francophones and Anglophones at the Middle Level of the Canadian Public Service (1965)

Francophones		Anglophones	
Type of School	Per Cent Attending	Type of School	Per Cent Attending
Classical College	33	English Public School (School Outside Quebec)	72
French Private School	23	English Private School	8
French Public School (in Quebec)	18	English Separate School (In Quebec or English Catholic Outside)	7
French Separate School (Publicly Supported Outside Quebec)	6	French System	0
English System	13	Other or Not Indicated	13
Other or Not Indicated	6		
Total	99	Total	100
	(N:128)		(N:168)

On the Francophone side there is diversity in the educational systems followed. Substantial groupings have emerged from several types of systems, the principal one being the Classical College. These colleges are run by the religious orders and concentrate their training in the humanities and liberal arts. Nearly a third of the Francophones are graduates of this system. More than a fifth (23 per cent) attended private schools. It is rather surprising that only 24 per cent received a public education in French and that 13 per cent went through the English system. There is less educational diversity among Anglophones. Seven in ten (73 per cent) attended the English public school system. Only a handful (9 per cent) have gone through private schools such as Upper Canada College, Ridley, or Trinity. None of the Anglophones received a considerable portion of his or her secondary education at French schools.

What impact these several educational channels have had can be partially seen by examining the careers which their graduates entered. For the Anglophones the effects seem to be minimal. Those of public and private school backgrounds are fairly evenly spread among the three career types with only a slight tendency for administrators to receive more public and fewer private-trained than the other two categories (Table 2.7). There is a stronger impact of educational stream on career choice among the Francophones. Those from Classical Colleges are over-represented in the professional-scientific category (Table 2.8). This is not surprising since a degree granted by a Classical College was ten or fifteen years ago a prerequisite for entering a French university. Both the other two career types draw more heavily from the private school system. Also of note is the substantial percentage—23 per cent—of administrators who have emerged from the English system. With a French background and English schooling, they would undoubtedly have bilingual skills that would be important for supervising employees. In fact, it is likely that the bilingual skill was instrumental in obtaining an administrative position.

What of the substance and quality of the education received by Francophones and Anglophones at the middle level? Earlier we reported that Anglophones have a slightly higher level of education than do Francophones. Further differences exist in educational specialization. As Figure 2.7 reveals, 68 per cent of Anglophones but only 39 per cent of Francophones who have gone to college or university have specialized in science or engineering. Francophones are more likely to have university training in arts, commerce, or law. This might suggest that Anglophones, possessors of a more "modern" technical education, can be expected to receive higher average salaries than Francophones. However, as Chapter 4 will reveal, the federal administration tends to reward those with a generalist education and policy-making or administrative skills as highly as those with science or engineering skills. Thus educational specializa-

TABLE 2.7

Type of Secondary School Attended by Anglophones at the Middle Level of the Canadian Public Service (1965) by Career Type

	Type of School			
Career Type	English Public	English Private	Other*	% Total
Professional and Scientific (N:84)	71	10	19	100
Technical and Semi-Professional (N:42)	71	12	17	100
Administrative (N:42)	79	5	17	101
Total (N:168)	72	8	20	100

* Includes those who attended English technical or separate schools, some "other" school, or for whom relevant information is not available.

TABLE 2.8

Type of Secondary School Attended by Francophones at the Middle Level of the Canadian Public Service (1965) by Career Type

	Type of School				
Career Type	Classical College	French Private	English System	Other*	% Total
Professional and Scientific (N:43)	44	12	12	33	101
Technical and Semi-Professional (N:54)	26	30	9	35	100
Administrative (N:31)	29	29	23	19	100
Total (N:128)	33	23	13	31	100

* Includes those who attended French public, technical, or separate schools, those from some "other" system, and ones for whom relevant information is not available.

FIGURE 2.7

Type of Educational Specialization of Francophones and Anglophones at the Middle Level of the Canadian Public Service (1965)*

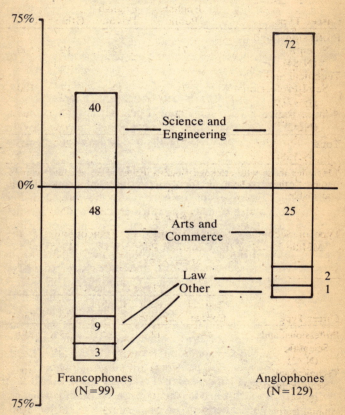

* Excludes those who have no university experience.

tion, by itself, ought not to put Francophones at a disadvantage.

The educational situation at the middle-level mirrors the output of Canadian Universities. English-Canadian universities compared to French-Canadian universities grant a much larger proportion of their degrees in science fields.[23] Thirty-three per cent of all Bachelor and first professional degrees granted by English-language institutions during 1962-65 were in "Natural Sciences" compared to 15.3 per cent of degrees from French-language institutions[24] during the same period.

Among the bureaucratic elite those with science and engineering backgrounds are not so dominant as they are at the middle level. In the elite, persons with specialized university training are fairly evenly distributed between the three areas of science and engineering, law, and the social sciences.[25] Of the 159 with degrees, 26 per cent had science or engineering degrees, 25 per cent law degrees, and 24 per cent a degree in one of the social sciences. The remaining 25 per cent had either general arts degrees or a specialty that could not be determined. Law, in particular, is not as prominent at the middle level as it is in the elite.

Another way of determining differences in the nature of the education obtained by Francophones and Anglophones is to examine the "prestige" of the universities they attended. For instance, in English Canada it is often argued, and sometimes demonstrated, that the top levels of business enterprises, universities, or the federal Public Service are the preserve of persons drawn from a short list of prestigious universities in Canada (Toronto, Queens, McGill), the United States (the "Ivy League"), or England (Oxford and Cambridge). This is certainly not the state of affairs at the middle level of the Public Service. Table 2.9 shows that four in ten of the Anglophones are from non-prestigious English Canadian universities and about the same proportion of Francophones are educated in non-prestigious French-Canadian universities. On the other hand, just over a quarter (26 per cent) of the Anglophones and —surprisingly—11 per cent of the Francophones went to one of the leading English-Canadian universities (Toronto, Queens, McGill). A fifth (22 per cent) of the University-educated Francophones come from one of the two major French-Canadian universities, Université de Montréal or Université Laval. A prestigious American or European centre figures in the university background of but 7 per cent of the Francophones and 13 per cent of the Anglophones. In short, half or more of both the Francophones and Anglophones with university experience have attended non-prestigious institutions either in Canada or abroad. This suggests that the Public Service is an especially congenial workplace for those who do not come from "name" universities.

It is evident that English-language universities have in the past placed more stress on scientific and technological fields thus producing a larger proportion of graduates with such training. Until recently these fields were relatively neglected in French-language or bilingual universities. The impact of the reforms launched in Quebec's higher education after 1960 came too late for the Francophones in this study. They are between 25 and 45 years of age and most obtained their higher education during the 1940's and 1950's. Many of these Francophones acknowledge the neglect and gave this as their reason for seeking training in science or engineering at English-language universities in Canada or the United States. Those who did so appear to have done better in both salary and promotions than those who completed all their university education in French-language institutions.[26]

The weakness of French-language scientific and technical training is one factor detrimental to Francophone advancement in the Public Service; so, it would appear, is the inadequacy of primary and secondary schooling for Francophones in Ottawa and other French-speaking parts of Ontario, if not in nearly all regions in Canada outside of the Province of Quebec, where there are concentrations of Francophones. For instance, in the Ontario secondary school system (including public, private, and separate schools) of those who speak French at home, 23 per cent entering Grade 9 continued in school for five years.[27] Of those entering Grade 9 speaking English at home, the percentage retained is twice as large, i.e., 47 per cent of the English group managed to stay in for five years. In Ottawa, the French-language group fared less well than in the province as a whole, while the English did markedly better. Fifth year enrolment for the French-language group was 20 per cent of the original enrolment while in the English-speaking group, 56 per cent of the Grade 9 entrants were still there 5 years later. Further, less than 2 per cent of the entering French-language group received the "Honour Graduation Diploma" for five years in a row of successfully-completed work, while 16 per cent of the English-language group did so.[28] The relative differences between language groups in Ontario as a whole and in Ottawa held up at all occupational levels. Not only among those whose fathers were "professionals" or "executives," but also among those of "farm" backgrounds, the proportion staying in secondary school for five years among the English-speaking students was consistently twice as high as the proportion in the French-speaking group. Since the federal administration relies so heavily on Franco-Ontarian recruitment, the upshot is that the Public Service contains a large corps of Francophones with limited educational backgrounds.

TABLE 2.9

Prestige of the Universities Attended by Francophones and Anglophones at the Middle Level of the Canadian Public Service (1965)*

Prestige of University	Francophones	Anglophones
Prestigious English Canadian (Toronto, Queens, McGill)	11	26
Other English Canadian	15	42
Prestigious French Canadian (Montréal, Laval)	22	0
Other French Canadian	39	1
Prestigious American (Ivy League, Chicago)	1	4
Prestigious European (Oxford, Cambridge, Sorbonne, Bordeau, Strasbourgh)	6	9
Other Foreign	7	18
Total	101 (N:88)	100 (N:125)

* Includes only those who attended university for more than 2 years.

In sum, it could be expected that certain areas of neglect in the educational systems of both Quebec and Ontario would lead to occupational disadvantages for Francophones. It is important not to push this point too far, however, for educational disadvantage is only one of a host of identifiable factors which could hold Francophone public servants back, as Chapters 4 and 5 make clear.

F. Work Experience Outside the Public Service

In an industrial society like Canada, to pursue a professional, technical or administrative career almost inevitably means to move: between regions of the country, between employers, between types of work. In the federal administration, some employees joined right after finishing their schooling and have stayed on in the same location and type of work. Many others have worked for another employer, sometimes a great variety of them, before entering the Public Service. Still others start off in the federal administration, but then shift between departments or cities, or leave for awhile and then return again. There are many variations on the movement theme. The result is that a government department receives many persons who have worked in various parts of the private sector or in other units of the federal administration and regularly releases many of its employees who depart for these work units.

The present section reports on the amount and type of working experience that civil servants have had in work-places "outside" the Public Service. Since my data are drawn from a survey taken at a single point in time, a cross-section of persons of varying ages is included. Thus this is a "snapshot" of the accumulated experiences in outside employment of current public servants including not only some who are well-launched on their careers but also some who have just entered the work world.

The average age of middle-level Anglophones at the time of joining the federal administration is 29.0 years; Francophones are somewhat younger at 26.4. As well, a majority in both linguistic groups enters some type of employment other than the federal Public Service immediately after finishing their schooling. This suggests that despite the extensive recruiting programmes of the Public Service aimed specifically at university students, most of the current middle-level employees started their careers elsewhere. There is a marked Francophone-Anglophone difference, however. Francophones are consider-

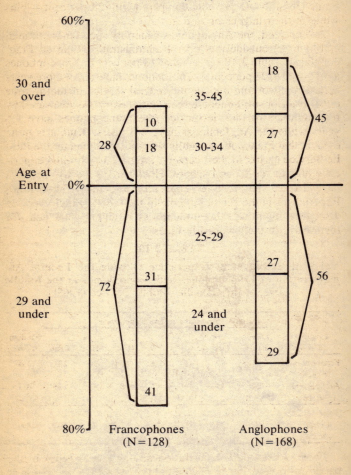

FIGURE 2.8

Age at Entry to the Federal Administration of Francophones and Anglophones at the Middle Level of the Canadian Public Service (1965)

ably more likely to enter the federal administration immediately after completing their schooling: 41 per cent did so compared with 24 per cent of the Anglophones. And, as Figure 2.8 indicates, a much larger proportion of Anglophones than Francophones—45 per cent compared with 28 per cent—joins while in their thirties or forties.

As expected, the Anglophones generally spend more time in employment outside the federal administration than do Francophones. Table 2.10 reveals that 12 per cent of Francophones as opposed to 21 per cent of Anglophones have ten or more years experience working outside the federal service including time either prior or subsequent to their initial entry. As measured by median years of outside service, the Francophones have 1.6 years while the Anglophones have 4.3 years. Thus it is quite evident that Francophone public servants tend to enter the Public Service earlier in their careers, after a fairly limited experience outside the federal sphere. However, as we will see in a later chapter, they tend to depart after a relatively short time. Experiences in the career systems of the federal Public Service discourage them and the attraction government work held for them early in their work-life fades.

TABLE 2.10

Years of Employment Experience Outside the Federal Administration of Francophones and Anglophones at the Middle Level of the Canadian Public Service (1965)

Linguistic Group	Years of Outside Experience						Total	Median Years
	Direct Entry	3 or Less	4-6	7-9	10-12	13 or More		
Francophones (N:128)	41	27	12	9	2	10	101	1.6
Anglophones (N:168)	24	23	16	17	8	13	101	4.3
Total Middle Level (N:296)	27	23	15	16	7	12	100	3.6

There is considerable variation among career types in the pattern of outside work (Table 2.11). In fact, the variation is such that the Francophone-Anglophone differential does not hold up across career types. Anglophone administrators, for instance, are more likely to enter government work directly

TABLE 2.11

Years of Employment Experience Outside the Federal Administration of Francophones and Anglophones at the Middle Level of the Canadian Public Service (1965) by Career Type

Linguistic Group and Career Type	Direct Entry	Years of Outside Experience						Median Years
		3 or Less	4-6	7-9	10-12	13 or more	Total	
Francophones								
Professional and Scientific (N:43)	51	23	12	5	0	9	100	1.0
Technical and Semi-Professional (N:54)	28	30	11	13	4	15	101	3.2
Administrative (N:31)	48	29	13	7	0	3	100	1.1
Anglophones								
Professional and Scientific (N:84)	19	24	19	13	13	12	100	4.8
Technical and Semi-Professional (N:42)	17	19	19	22	5	19	101	6.5
Administrative (N:42)	41	31	5	10	5	10	102	2.0

from school than are the Francophone technical and semi-professional employees. This Anglophone career type also has less outside experience than the Francophone type as indicated by median years of service. Thus, one category of Francophone careerist has more outside experience than one category of Anglophones; the difference between linguistic groups does not cut across all career types.

Interestingly, it is the technical and semi-professional employees in both linguistic groups who have had the most extensive outside experience. To be more precise, it is principally the technicians who have had lengthy work histories outside, as Table 2.12 shows. One type of professional, the engineer, also has a relatively extensive period of outside work. On the other hand, it is the lower administrators in both linguistic groups who tend to join the federal administration after short sojourns or none at all in other employment settings. However, Francophone scientists have the least outside experience of all careerists. Eight in ten of them entered government employment as soon as they had finished their schooling. Since Anglophone scientists experience longer periods of outside employment it would seem that either the Francophone scientists are more restricted in their career movements or are more strongly attracted to federal employment, or both.

The differences in outside experience among the career types also is reflected in differences between departments. The Department of Public Works with its preponderance of technical and engineering employees contains relatively more people who have developed lengthy work histories in work settings outside the federal. The majority of the Anglophones interviewed are late arrivals to government service. Secretary of State, with its concentration of engineers in the Patent Office, also registers a relatively high proportion of persons with lengthy outside service among both its Anglophone and Francophone personnel. By contrast, among the Francophones in Agriculture there is but a meagre store of experiences accumulated in outside employment, largely to be accounted for by the high direct entry rate of Francophone scientists. Thus, departmental differences are largely a product of their career-type composition.

TABLE 2.12

Median Years and Per Cent with Ten Years or More of Employment Experience Outside the Federal Administration of Francophones and Anglophones at the Middle Level of the Canadian Public Service (1965) by Career Type

Career Type	Francophones			Anglophones		
	Median Years	Per Cent With 10 Years or More	N*	Median Years	Per Cent With 10 Years or More	N*
Scientists	0.6	7	14	3.5	14	35
Senior Policy-Makers	0.9	12	17	2.8	24	25
Semi-Professionals	2.1	16	51	5.0	14	28
Engineers	4.0	8	12	5.0	30	40
Technicians	4.5	17	18	9.2	38	21
Lower Administrators	1.4	0	16	1.3	11	19
Total	1.6	12	128	4.3	21	168

* This is the case base on which the per cent is computed.

Geographical Moves

Forty-six per cent of those at the middle level have moved themselves, and their families if any, from one area to another two or more times in the course of their work outside the government[29] (Table 2.13). Since this figure applies only to persons at mid-career, it grossly understates the amount of movement that these people will have experienced by the end of their work lives. However, it is indicative of the sort of shifting about that persons go through early in their work lives while trying to establish a secure position for themselves.

TABLE 2.13

Number of Geographical Moves During Employment Outside the Federal Administration of Francophones and Anglophones at the Middle Level of the Canadian Public Service (1965)

Linguistic Group	Number of Geographical Moves				
	None	One	Two	Three or More	% Total
Francophones (N:128)	42	31	15	12	100
Anglophones (N:168)	24	26	17	33	100
Total Middle Level (N:296)	27	26	17	29	99

At first glance, there appears to be large linguistic variation. The Francophones are more likely to have no geographic moves and the Anglophones to have three or more. However, the difference is minimized, although it does not disappear, when we control for the extent of outside experience (Table 2.14). Among the early entrants to government service, there is no major difference between Anglophones and Francophones in their movement experiences. It is only among those with lengthy periods of outside work that the Anglophones are more mobile. The Anglophones who enter the federal administration when they are over 30 have moved around much more than their

Francophone counterparts. Thus, among both Francophones and Anglophones who enter the government at an early age there is an equally small proportion of persons who moved around a great deal, while the Anglophones who enter later in their careers contain a higher proportion of those who have moved a considerable amount than do the Francophones.

TABLE 2.14

Number of Geographical Moves During Employment Outside the Federal Administration of Francophones and Anglophones at the Middle Level of the Canadian Public Service (1965) by Age at Entry

Age At Entry and Linguistic Group	Number of Geographical Moves				
	None	One	Two	Three or More	% Total
Age 29 or Less At Entry					
Francophones (N:92)	48	33	12	8	101
Anglophones (N:94)	39	38	13	10	100
Age 30 to 45 At Entry					
Francophones (N:36)	28	28	22	22	100
Anglophones (N:74)	4	15	22	60	101

One obvious fact that explains the greater percentage of immobile Francophones is the large proportion raised in the Ottawa-Hull area (43 per cent of all Francophones). Of these, four in ten entered the federal administration directly after finishing their education. As many of them reported, it was the natural thing for those raised in the capital region to do. Surprisingly, however, a *larger* proportion (49 per cent) of those raised in Montreal or other parts of Quebec (excluding Hull) reported that they came directly from an educational institution into federal employment.

Anglophones from the capital region mentioned the same

process as the Francophones but not as many came directly to the government. Thirteen per cent worked for nine years or more outside the federal Public Service but a third entered directly. This contrasts to the lower score of 19 per cent of Anglophones from Western Canada who directly entered the federal administration. Hence, Anglophones from the Ottawa-Hull area are more prone to go directly from school to government service than are Anglophones from other regions, but Francophones, no matter the part of the country they are raised in, enter directly more frequently than any Anglophone group.

Job-Switching

Among those who did have outside working experience, I was also interested in the number of job changes and the amount of disruption to personal life that these changes caused. In other words, my concern was the dimension of orderliness-disorderliness: the incidence of discontinuity experienced by each respondent in his occupational history *before* joining the Public Service. The resulting measure took account of the number of moves between different organizations, each move classified as to whether the person (1) continued to do roughly the same sort of work or (2) made a clean break and started on a quite different occupation. Obviously, the latter type of move was indicative of greater disorder. As well, a control for number of years of outside work was built into the measure. This meant that a person who made several moves over a long period of time would be regarded as switching jobs in a more orderly fashion than someone who made the same number and type of moves within a short period. The resulting measure wh·n applied to the two linguistic groups in the federal administration is seen in table 2.15.[30]

There is no gross Anglophone-Francophone difference in disruptive working experiences outside the federal administration. The majority of both groups shift jobs in an orderly fashion or with only slight disorder. Only 7 per cent of the Francophones and 5 per cent of the Anglophones have undergone extremely disruptive changes. And the ranks of those with very disorderly work histories are over-represented by those in certain careers.

TABLE 2.15

Incidence of Disorderly Job-Switching Experienced by Those With Employment Outside the Federal Administration Among Francophones and Anglophones at the Middle Level of the Canadian Public Service (1965)

Linguistic Group	Incidence of Disorderly Job-Switching				
	Orderly	Slight Disorder	Medium Disorder	High Disorder	% Total
Francophones (N:76)	22	57	15	7	101
Anglophones (N:128)	16	59	20	5	100
Total Middle Level (N:204)	17	59	20	5	101

Among the Anglophones, there are relatively few professionals and scientists who have had a chaotic work history before joining (Table 2.16). It is principally the technical, semi-professional, and administrative employees who do so. On the Francophone side, it is rare indeed to find professionals and scientists, and also, administrators, whose early work history is marked by considerable switching between unrelated jobs. It is only the technical and semi-professional employees who have such experiences. In fact, one type in this category of personnel—the Translator—has the most varied previous work history of all the careerists in both linguistic groups. More than four in ten of them (8 of 19) have a work history that is either medium or high in disorderliness. To a certain extent this outcome flows from the type of man attracted to the work (often men who have failed at careers in journalism, law, or the church), and in the nature of translation tasks: the work requires considerable intellectual skill yet often is routine and boring and, hence, is a "last resort" sort of job. In addition, demands for translation services have risen sharply in recent years, yet most departments still regard this work as a nuisance—merely an added cost in time and money of carrying out the government's business; something to be avoided when possible. In short, the type of work and status it offers means that a translator's post is sought out mainly by persons who have failed in "better" careers or who have left a field for personal reasons, but, in any case, have had an unsettling experience and are in dire need of employment and security.

TABLE 2.16

Incidence of Medium and High Disorderly Job-Switching Experienced by Those With Employment Outside the Federal Administration Among Francophones and Anglophones at the Middle Level of the Canadian Public Service (1965) by Career Type

	Francophones		Anglophones	
Career Type	Per Cent Medium or High in Disorder	N*	Per Cent Medium or High in Disorder	N*
Professional and Scientific	10	21	18	68
Technical and Semi-Professional	36	39	34	35
Administrative	0	16	32	25
Total	21	76	25	128

* These are the bases on which the percentages are computed.

A close examination of the work histories of those who obtained their first employment outside the Public Service indicated that for a small group the decision to join the Public Service often came after the experience of sharp, sometimes unpredictable disruption of ties to job or local community (e.g., after precipitously quitting a job for personal reasons, after a job lay-off, or after immigration). For this type of employee the Public Service often becomes a type of refuge—a place which held few prospects for advancement, but did provide a stable and undemanding employment situation. Such persons are located in the ranks of the 21 per cent of Francophones and 25 per cent of Anglophones who experienced medium or high disorder in their work history outside federal circles. (It should be recalled, however, that those with outside work histories either medium or high in disorder represent but 12.5 per cent of *all* Francophones and 19 per cent of *all* Anglophones, i.e., those with and without outside work experience). Thus a significant minority come to the federal administration not so much to build a career as to stabilize their occupational situation after defeat, disappointment or termination of communal ties. Francophones are less likely to have this experience. Although the Francophones who are employed outside the Public Service are as buffeted as their Anglophone counterparts, relatively fewer of them seek outside employment in the first place. In general, Francophones join the federal Public Service earlier in life. Anglophones, with their greater employment opportunities in the Canadian economy, are prone to work first in the private sector rather than come directly from school. However, once in, Anglophones stay on; Francophones join earlier but are much more likely to leave soon after their arrival, as we shall see.

G. Summary and Conclusions

The federal administration is a relatively open and talent-hungry organization at the middle level. It draws amply from native stock and newcomers to Canada, from all geographical regions except Quebec, a variety of ethnic-religious strains, urban and rural areas, and, with some favouring of the top levels, the several social classes in the country. Certainly the theme of heterogeneity is well demonstrated for the middle level. This is particularly evident in the contrasts made between it and the elite.

John Porter argues that the homogeneity of the bureaucratic elite may lead to a common ideology and sense of exclusiveness.

These senior public servants have, by and large, a common background in the social class and educational systems of Canada. Their high level of education and their link with the universities would suggest commonly held intellectual values. . . . There are many areas of formal and informal interaction common to, and at times exclusive to, the bureaucratic elite. For one thing, they live in a relatively small and occupationally homogeneous city. In their formal roles they come together in a large number of inter-departmental committees at home and abroad . . . Senior civil servants consult with one another, and for this purpose the informal settings at dinners, receptions, and evening parties are as important as the formally constituted committees. . . . the higher bureaucracy has some cohesiveness as a group and an orientation to intellectual values, particularly among those concerned with economic and social policy.[31]

This homogeneous body presides over a rather heterogeneous middle level. But already we can gather some impressions about the careerists who are likely to move quickly upward through the intermediate ranks into the elite.

The Francophones are clearly at a disadvantage. This is seen in various ways: the under-representation of persons of French descent at the middle level, the lower rate of recruitment from the province of Quebec, the lack of Roman Catholics, largely to be accounted for by the absence of French Catholics. Some of the Francophone disadvantage results from the inaccessibility of educational facilities of the sort that could equip them with appropriate skills. A second factor is that Francophones have a lower motivation to serve in the federal administration. The cultural character of the Public Service or the political ends it serves, or both, does not appeal to them.

In the closing pages of this chapter, I will discuss these two points further.

Much has been said in this chapter about the type of education available to Francophones; here we want to temper these remarks slightly. For it is a popular argument in English Canada to attribute the lack of Francophones in the upper reaches of the public and private sectors to an educational system unfitted for the modern world. John Porter gives this view some scientific support in a comparison of provincial educational systems:

The least adequate educational facilities for an industrial society, as census data later presented show, have been those of Quebec where education for French Catholics has been not only costly but at the secondary level concentrated within the tradition of the classical college.[32]

Classical colleges, it seems, did not until recently emphasize science and technology, necessary fields for moving into the world of industry. Then, Porter adds a thought about the lack of Francophones in the federal bureaucratic elite: "It must be remembered, however, that French-Canadian education has not provided a large reservoir of administrators who could eventually be promoted to the higher levels."[33] This carries the argument a little too far. It is hard to judge what is a "large reservoir" but certainly the classical colleges have turned out a steady flow of persons with training in the liberal arts and the professions—exactly the stuff of which administrators are made. Remarking on the new emphasis on science in Quebec colleges and universities Nathan Keyfitz writes:

> As one offers the old system a regretful salute and farewell, however, one notes that it teaches a curriculum similar to that which formed many an empire-builder at Oxford before he went out to India to be the absolute ruler of a district containing a million people, or to London to start climbing to the chairmanship of a large railway or bank.[34]

Yet, if the classical colleges have long turned out persons with administrative capacity, why does the view persist that the French-Catholic educational system is in an abysmal state? We seem to be in the presence of a defensive overstatement about French-Canadian education. It permits English Canadians to avoid explaining the absence of the French from positions of power in terms of English resistance or even discrimination, and to shift the blame to the French Canadians themselves. Anglophones assume that when French Canadians get better educations and strive harder, they will make it. This denies the fact that there already is an untapped source of able Francophones available for government work or that the culture of large work organizations systematically excludes Francophones who do not fit "English" slots.

It is not strictly education but rather language and culture which are the real issues. In the senior reaches of the federal government and most large companies, English is the language of work. Competence in the use of language and the expression of ideas is valued among managers. A person working in a language not his own is at a disadvantage from the start. A French candidate

> is genuinely unable to do the work as well as the English candidate wherever that work consists in large part in the manipulation of symbols in English. To say otherwise would be to assert that French Canadians are capable of learning to speak and think in English as well as the English themselves.[35]

Although this may well happen to some Francophones, most of those who retain any semblance of a French Canadian identity do not have complete confidence in and competence with English. This means that they are systematically barred from high office. Either as a result of the uncertainty of Anglophone senior managers about the competence of Francophones or outright indifference, the Francophones have not fared well in large-scale organizations. Finally, limited opportunities for incumbents produce limited motivation among potential recruits. Young Francophones observe that their elders meet resistance in certain careers and organizations, and they choose their own fields of training and work in this light. Thus the barriers posed by the use of English and occupational and organizational choices of Francophones reinforce each other; the result is the underrepresentation of Francophones in various careers and work places.

This brief aside contains themes that will be developed in much greater detail in later chapters. The themes have been introduced at this juncture to indicate that laying the major blame on French Canadian education for the failure of Francophones to become economic successes in Canada is too simple-minded. Despite this *caveat*, it is nevertheless the case that the emphasis of Quebec education in the 1940's and 1950's and the lack of success of Francophones in the educational system of Ontario have meant that a large proportion of Francophones were poorly-equipped for working in the federal administration.

As to attraction toward work in the federal government, a national interview study conducted by the Social Research Group of Montreal contained enquiries about people's perceptions of job opportunities available at the federal level.[36] It asked whether the respondent felt that English Canadians have more chances, French Canadians have more chances, or whether all have an equal chance of getting the "top" jobs in the federal government. Thirty-six per cent of the total sample felt that persons from all ethnic groups have equal opportunity. However, significantly fewer French Canadians (18 per cent) felt that there was equal opportunity. Also, while 38 per cent of all respondents felt that English Canadians have more chances for the best jobs, 62 per cent of the French respondents felt that this was the case. Only 4 per cent of the total sample and 2.5 per cent of the French respondents felt that French Canadians have more chances. French Canadians, then, are much more prone than other respondents to think that English Canadians have more chances than other groups of getting the best jobs in the federal administration.[37] On the grounds of perceived work opportunities alone, the French are less likely to consider federal employment. When added to this is the prospect for many of moving to Ottawa and having to live and work much of the time in English surroundings, it is not surprising that they are less highly motivated to join the federal Public Service.

A national survey of Canadian youth 13 to 20 years of age provides further supportive findings.[38] The young people were queried about their attitudes toward different levels of government. One question asked: "Which government would be best to work for—if the salary was the same on each job?" The results are presented in Table 2.17.

Both groups of non-French youth rated the federal government highest as a congenial working environment. These same two groups also rated their provincial governments lowest on this standard. This indicates that the English and other language groups view the provincial government as the one least attractive to work for. On the other hand, the French-speaking youth regard the provincial government as the most promising employer and rated the federal government on a par with local government.

The same study found regional and age differences in attitudes toward the three levels of government. The French from Quebec held much more negative views of the federal government than other groups. The strongest positive feelings for a

TABLE 2.17

Orientation to Different Levels of Government by Language Spoken at Home Among Canadian Youth Between 13 and 20 Years of Age in 1965

Which government would be best to work for — if the salary was the same on each job?	Language Spoken At Home		
	English	French	Other
The government of your city, town or township	28	27	27
The government of your province	22	34	19
The government of Canada	39	28	38
I'm not sure	11	11	16
Total	100% (N:793)*	100% (N:529)*	100% (N:37)*

* All percentages computed from weighted case bases. These are the unweighted bases.

Source: John W. C. Johnstone, *Young People's Images of Canadian Society*, Table 1-15.

provincial government were registered by the English of British Columbia followed by the Quebec French. However, unlike the French Quebecers who downgraded the federal government, the British Columbia English directed negative sentiments towards local government.

Unlike the French Quebec youth, the English Quebecers gave the provincial government a negative evaluation. The Quebec English saw their primary source of positive aid located at the federal level.

In both the English and French groups increasing age is correlated with higher positive ratings for the provincial government. Among the French, increased age is also associated with increasing negative views of the federal government. It becomes clear, then, that as French youth approach the age when they enter the work world, the federal government is increasingly seen as an unattractive workplace.

It is evident, therefore, that differentials in education and motivation reduce the numbers of Francophones who come forward for federal employment. Nevertheless, we do find a sizeable contingent of Francophones at the middle level, and for four out of ten of them, the federal Public Service was their first employer after leaving school. Clearly these men, either out of interest or necessity, find the federal government a worthy employer. There was some suggestion that careers in science and lower-administration were especially likely to contain Francophones coming directly to government work from an educational institution.

Among those who worked outside the federal administration, I find that there are relatively few who experienced an unstable work life. Professionals and scientists especially show an orderly sequence of posts in their work outside government circles. It is technical and semi-professional workers in both Anglophone and Francophone groups who are especially prone to discontinuity in their worklife outside the Public Service. As the next chapter reveals, the motivation to enter the federal service is greatly affected by the type of career one is in and by whether or not one's work experience outside the federal sphere was stable or unstable.

The above also provides support for Hypothesis 1: minority men are drawn from a narrow area around the federal capital; they are generally of lower social origins than majority men; they have less extensive educational experiences; and for most federal employment was their first work experience.

Notes

[1]These are the more recent studies: *Australia*—H. A. Scarrow, *The Higher Public Service of the Commonwealth of Australia* (Durham, N.C., 1957), and the findings reviewed by Kurt B. Mayer, "Social Stratification in Two Equalitarian Societies: Australia and the United States," *Social Research*, 31 (Winter, 1964), 435-65; *Britain*—R. K. Kelsall, *Higher Civil Servants in Britain* (London, 1955), and several essays in William A. Robson, (ed.), *The Civil Service in Britain and France* (New York, 1956); *Egypt*—Morroe Berger, *Bureaucracy and Society in Modern Egypt* (Princeton, 1957); *Germany*—Ralf Dahrendorf, *Society and Democracy in Germany* (Garden City, N.Y., 1967); *India*—V. Subramaniam, "Representative Bureaucracy: A Reassess-

ment,'' *American Political Science Review*, 61 (December, 1967), 1010-9; *Japan*—Akira Kubota, *Higher Civil Servants in Postwar Japan* (Princeton, 1969); *Pakistan*—Muneer Ahmad, *The Civil Servant in Pakistan* (Karachi, 1964); *United States*—Reinhard Bendix, *Higher Civil Servants in American Society* (Boulder, Colo., 1949); W. Lloyd Warner *et al.*, *The American Federal Executive* (New Haven, 1963), and David T. Stanley, *The Higher Civil Service* (Washington, 1964).

[2]The study originally appeared as ''Higher Public Servants and the Bureaucratic Elite in Canada,'' *Canadian Journal of Economics and Political Science*, 24 (November, 1958), 483-501. It provides the basis for Chapter 14 of John Porter, *The Vertical Mosaic: An Analysis of Social Class and Power in Canada* (Toronto, 1965). Future references in my study will be to the latter, more accessible, source.

[3]Porter, *Vertical Mosaic*, p. 612.

[4]Many results are reported separately for this group.

[5]Peter C. Newman, ''The Ottawa Establishment,'' *Maclean's*, August 22, 1964.

[6]Eugene Forsey, ''Parliament is Endangered by Mr. King's Principle,'' *Saturday Night*, October 9, 1949, pp. 10-1 and J. E. Hodgetts, ''The Liberal and the Bureaucrat,'' *Queen's Quarterly*, 62, (Summer, 1955), pp. 176-83.

[7]John Meisel, ''The Formulation of Liberal and Conservative Programmes in the 1957 Canadian General Election,'' *Canadian Journal of Economics and Political Science*, 26 (November, 1960), pp. 565-74.

[8]For the first time I refer to findings based on the aggregation of the samples from the five departments. To obtain the results for both the total middle level and for all Anglophones it was necessary to go through a weighting process. For the total middle level it was necessary to give the Anglophone samples extra weight since they represented larger numbers of personnel than did the Francophone samples. In four out of five departments, all Francophones were interviewed, while in every department the Anglophone sample represented a substantial number of persons.

Much the same logic was applied to obtaining results for all Anglophones. The departmental samples which represented a large number of persons were given extra weight while samples from small populations were devalued when combining the results from the five departments.

All subsequent results in the text and tables have been weighted where appropriate. The weighting process is described in more detail in Appendix 1.

[9]Porter, *Vertical Mosaic*, p. 442. It should be added that Porter's

results are drawn from information about 202 of the 243 elite members.

[10]*Ibid.*, p. 443.

[11]*Ibid.*, Chap. 2.

[12]*Ibid.*, p. 422.

[13]*Ibid.*, p. 443.

[14]*Ibid.*, p. 443.

[15]*Ibid.*, p. 443.

[16]For further details beyond those presented in this paragraph see Appendix 2.

[17]See the review of data in Porter, *Vertical Mosaic*, Chap. 6.

[18]*Ibid.*, p. 444.

[19]*Ibid.*, p. 445.

[20]*Ibid.*, p. 433.

[21]*Ibid.*, p. 433.

[22]*Ibid.*, p. 435.

[23]Herbert Taylor, "The Output of Canadian Universities and Colleges, 1962-65," Ottawa: The Royal Commission on Bilingualism and Biculturalism, (Internal Research Report), 1966.

[24]The total of Bachelor and first professional degrees granted by French-language institutions includes here "les baccalauréats es arts" from Classical Colleges. When these degrees are excluded the proportion of science degrees rises to 25.4 per cent.

[25]Porter, *Vertical Mosaic*, p. 434.

[26]Of course, those Francophones who obtain university training in English rather than French-language institutions obtain advantages other than simply superior training. In the first place their fluency in English improves; in the second, their ability to adapt to an English-speaking work environment also increases. Finally they received degrees from universities which were prestigious in the eyes of the dominant Anglophone group in the federal Public Service.

[27]The findings in this paragraph are from A. J. C. King and Carol E. Angi, *Language and Secondary School Success*, Ottawa: The Royal Commission on Bilingualism and Biculturalism (Internal Research Report), 1966.

[28]A number of students in both language groups who missed or failed a year obtained the Diploma after a period of more than five years.

[29]Note that a move away from one region to join a unit of the federal Public Service is considered as a geographical move here. These are fairly rare occurrences, however; most of the moves took place between units which were both outside the federal sphere.

[30]Appendix 2 contains exact details of the construction of this variable. The theoretical relevance of the orderliness-disorderliness dimension of work history is explained by Harold L. Wilensky, "Orderly Careers and Social Participation: The Impact of Work History on

Social Integration in the Middle Mass," *American Sociological Review*, 26 (August, 1961), pp. 521-39.

[31]Porter, *Vertical Mosaic*, pp. 447-8.

[32]*Ibid.*, p. 169.

[33]*Ibid.*, p. 442.

[34]Nathan Keyfitz, "Canadians and Canadiens," *Queen's Quarterly*, 70 (Winter, 1963), p. 173.

[35]*Ibid.*, p. 171.

[36]The Social Research Group, *A Study of Inter-Ethnic Relations in Canada*, Ottawa: Royal Commission on Bilingualism and Biculturalism (Internal Research Report), 1965.

[37]*Ibid.*, p. 76.

[38]John W. C. Johnstone, *Young People's Images of Canadian Society, An Opinion Survey of Canadian Youth 13 to 20 Years of Age* (Ottawa, 1969).

Chapter Three

Joining the Federal Administration

The previous chapter indicates that most men entering the middle level of the federal administration proceed along standard, socially structured routes. Forty-one per cent of Francophones and 24 per cent of Anglophones come directly into the federal service from an educational institution. If they start below the middle level, they work their way up through conventional career routes. Among those who work elsewhere before entry, three-quarters of both Anglophones and Francophones experience a fairly orderly sequence of jobs. Both early and later entrants, therefore, have quite stable and structured lives at school or work before starting along the stable and structured career routes of the federal administration.

What attracts these men to bureaucratic careers? In the course of the interview they were asked to give their main reasons for joining the federal Public Service. The following are the most prominent:

(1) Career Opportunities—the work appeared attractive and the chances for promotion, for assuming a position of responsibility, or for making a high salary looked good.

(2) Unique Field—the federal administration was the only place or one of the few places in which to pursue a specialized interest.

(3) Training Experience—the job provided an opportunity to learn new skills that would be useful in the future, often in a career outside the public sector.

(4) Public Service—a desire to do valuable and important work and serve the "public good" could be fulfilled.

(5) Security—the federal service offered job security, a steady income, good working hours, or low pressure.

(6) Ottawa-Hull Attraction—the federal government was

the main employer in the Capital Region and the person wanted to stay in the area or to return to it after being away for some time.

(7) Only Job—the federal administration made the only acceptable offer at a time when immediate employment was a necessity.

(8) Language—a few Francophones either wanted to work in French in a unit where that language predominated or saw government employment as an opportunity to learn English.

The above categories were developed in the course of interviewing, and later, reviewing responses to the questions about entering the federal administration. In addition, the categories were shaped by the theory of work motivation. Sociologists have been concerned for some time about identifying the things that men seek in their work. A fundamental distinction appears in the theoretical and empirical literature. Some workers mainly emphasize the nature of the work itself, the presence or absence of opportunities for applying their knowledge or learning new skills; others are chiefly concerned with security, or other factors not directly related to the work. The latter mainly revolve about the benefits provided by the employing organization. Entry motivations of the former type— represented by reasons (1) to (4) above—were termed *work* factors; the latter, as seen in reasons (5) to (8), were called *benefit* factors.

Before presenting my findings, I will review in more depth the nature and relevance of the distinction between work and benefit factors.

A. Work and Benefit Factors

The distinction between work and benefit factors, or to put it in a more general way, between factors related to the *content* of the work and those bearing on the *context* in which work is done, has appeared in several guises in the sociological literature. In a study published in 1954 of a federal agency responsible for coordinating and subsidizing defense research in the United States, Dwaine Marvick distinguished between two constellations of factors important in work.[1] One constellation consisted of "task" factors, the other of "benefit" factors. Employees concerned with task factors gave special emphasis to opportunities for learning new skills, trying out ideas, or making full use of their abilities. The focus was on job content and the possibilities of enjoyment offered by the work. Concern with benefit factors meant an emphasis on the by-products of working in an organization: security, salary, advancement, and prestige in the community, among others. Marvick compared the civil and military administrators—he calls them "institutionalists"—to the "specialists." He found that specialists were more likely to value task factors than were institutionalists. Conversely, institutionalists were more prone to emphasize benefit factors than were specialists.

Herzberg and his colleagues reviewed the literature on job satisfaction and other job attitudes published through 1954.[2] With this background, the Herzberg group conducted a seminal piece of research published in 1959 with the title, *The Motivation to Work*.[3] The main focus was on 203 engineers and accountants in nine companies in Pittsburgh. The respondents were asked to provide stories about times that they felt either exceptionally good or exceptionally bad about their work. In the course of analysis of the stories, it emerged that those factors which made people happy with their work were different from the factors that made people unhappy with their work.

> When our respondents reported feeling happy with their jobs, they most frequently described factors related to their tasks, to events that indicated to them that they were successful in the performance of their work, and to the possibility of professional growth. Conversely, when feelings of unhappiness were reported, they were not associated with the job itself but with conditions that surround the doing of the job.[4]

In particular, company policy and administrative procedures and the quality of supervision appeared to be the key sources of dissatisfaction. In short, these accountants and engineers appear to distinguish between factors associated with the content of the work (intrinsic factors) and factors in the work setting (extrinsic factors). The degree of satisfaction with work was an outcome of weighing these two sets of factors.

Similar results for managers are reported in a survey carried out by Porter.[5] The study included several levels of management from first-level supervisors to company presidents, in a great variety of firms throughout the United States. There was an effort to measure the degree of satisfaction of needs ranging from the basic security and social needs (to give help, to develop friendships) through the needs for esteem, autonomy, and self-actualization. Satisfaction of security and social needs was roughly equal across all levels of management, but reported satisfaction of esteem, autonomy, and self-actualization needs increased at each higher management level. Apparently, managers feel quite satisfied with security and social arrangements, but lower-level managers did not receive as many chances to obtain esteem, autonomy, and self-actualization as they desired. The main interest in this review, however, is that a distinction between a security-benefit syndrome and a work content syndrome emerges from the study.

In yet another study, this time of scientists and engineers, Friedlander and Walton found that decisions to leave an organization and expressions of dissatisfaction with the work resulted mainly from perceived problems in the work environment, while high satisfaction with work and decisions to stay on a job were related to reports of opportunities for self-development and challenging assignments.[6] The general theme, it appears, of this research and the work of Herzberg and his colleagues, is that work satisfaction resulted mainly from opportunities for self-expression, creativity, and personal growth. The report by Robert Blauner about levels of alienation among workers in four industries gives further weight to this contention.[7] Friedlander, however, challenged this theme in a more recent article.[8] He asserts that self-development and other such work factors may be important to professional and managerial people, but not to those in blue-collar jobs. His research bears this out. Clear-cut differences between white-collar and blue-collar employees appear. White-collar workers in the sample underlined the importance of work characteristics which satisfy needs for self-actualization while the predominant value among the blue-collar group was on environmental features that fulfill security needs and encourage smooth interpersonal relations. Occupational culture, therefore, is an important determinant of whether one will chiefly value features of the work itself or value aspects of the setting in which work is done.

The foregoing indicates that the distinction between work (content) and benefit (context) factors offers an important perspective for the sociology of careers. It ought to be helpful in examining the motives that propel men into federal employment.

B. Variations in Reasons for Joining

Anglophone personnel are generally more oriented toward their work and the creative aspects of their employment than are Francophones (Table 3.1). Fifty-two per cent of Anglophones join for work reasons as against 33 per cent among the Francophones. In particular, relatively more Anglophones are attracted by the career opportunities available and the possibilities of doing specialized work, often unique to the federal service. On the other hand, although a larger proportion of Francophones are concerned about organizational benefits, there is still a sizeable contingent of Anglophones who view the federal administration as a haven of security.

Figure 3.1 verifies that it is the professional and scientific workers in both linguistic groups who most desire creative work. The linguistic difference persists, however. Within each broad career type a larger proportion of Anglophones than Francophones joins the Public Service because of the attraction of the work. The difference is especially marked among those in technical and semi-professional careers. Here, the Anglophones are almost as strongly motivated by their work as are their fellows in professional-scientific fields. More than half the Anglophones name work factors, but only 29 per cent of the Francophones do so. Among administrators the linguistic difference is considerably less sharply drawn. Thus, the main points are that those in professional and scientific careers are especially likely to find the federal Public Service a congenial place in terms of the opportunities for creative work it offers; those in administrative careers and Francophones in technical

TABLE 3.1

Main Reason for Joining the Federal Administration of Francophones and Anglophones at the Middle Level of the Canadian Public Service (1965)

Main Reason for Joining	Linguistic Group		Total Middle Level
	Franco-phones	Anglo-phones	
Career Opportunities	17	23	22
Unique Field	9	20	18
Training Experience	6	7	6
Public Service	1	2	2
TOTAL WORK FACTORS	33	52	48
Security	19	23	22
Ottawa-Hull Attraction	12	8	8
Only Job	22	9	11
Language	2	0	0
TOTAL BENEFIT FACTORS	55	40	41
Other Reasons or Not Determined	13	9	10
	101 (N:128)	101 (N:168)	99 (N:296)

and semi-professional fields are especially drawn to the Public Service for its benefits; and in every career type, the Anglophones are more motivated by work factors than are Francophones.

A rough ordering of careers according to the proportion of persons they contain who join the government for the work going on there is provided in Figure 3.2. The ordering pertains in both linguistic groups. Scientists and senior policy-makers are most likely to enter government service for work factors. They are followed in order by semi-professionals, engineers, technicians, and last of all, lower administrators. The position of the engineers is slightly anomalous. As a professional group it would be expected that they would be high in their desire for creative work. Instead, they stand below the semi-professionals. It appears, then, that government engineers are

FIGURE 3.1

Main Reason for Joining the Federal Administration of Francophones and Anglophones at the Middle Level of the Canadian Public Service (1965) by Career Type

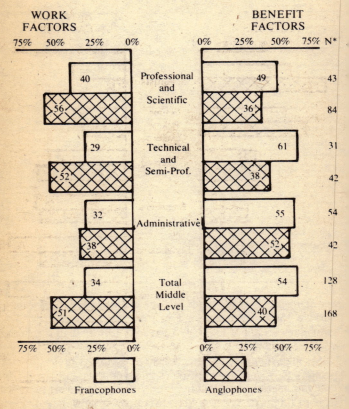

* This is the base on which the percentage joining for either work or benefit factors is calculated.

FIGURE 3.2

Main Reason for Joining the Federal Administration of Francophones and Anglophones at the Middle Level of the Canadian Public Service (1965) by Career Type

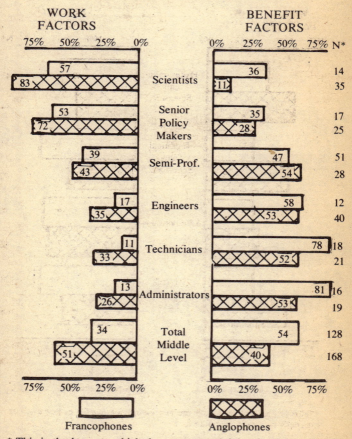

* This is the base on which the percentage joining for either work or benefit factors is calculated.

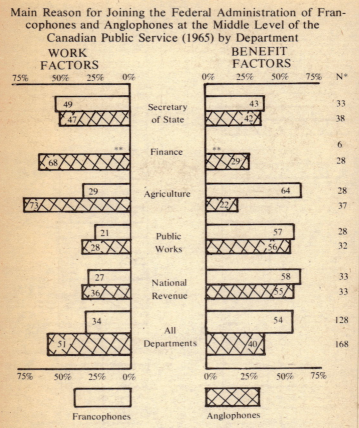

FIGURE 3.3

Main Reason for Joining the Federal Administration of Francophones and Anglophones at the Middle Level of the Canadian Public Service (1965) by Department

WORK FACTORS		Department	BENEFIT FACTORS		N*
49		Secretary of State	43		33
47			42		38
**		Finance	**		6
68			29		28
29		Agriculture	64		28
73			22		37
21		Public Works	57		28
28			56		32
27		National Revenue	58		33
36			55		33
34		All Departments	54		128
51			40		168

Francophones ☐   Anglophones ⊠

* This is the base on which the percentage joining for either work or benefit factors is calculated.
** Too few cases to estimate.

especially prone to view their employer as offering security and stable employment. The extreme examples of this, however, are the Françophone technicians and lower administrators among whom approximately eight in ten enter the federal administration to take advantage of the fringe benefits it affords.

It is important to note again that in every career category the Anglophones are more concerned about the quality of government work than are their Francophone colleagues.

In these two variables—linguistic group and career type—we seem to have arrived at strategic tools for dissecting work settings in the Public Service. The nature of the careers they contain will tell a great deal about their ethos. Also, within any specific career it can be expected that the Anglophone group contains a larger proportion of persons who entered in search of creative work than in the Francophone group.

In addition to the influence of language and career, organizational ethos is related to job motivation. In four out of five departments there is a similar orientation to work expressed by members of the two linguistic groups, as Figure 3.3 reveals. Fringe benefits are highly and equally relevant to both language groups in Public Works, National Revenue, and Secretary of State. This reveals much about the essential character of these departments. Since they perform routine service functions, few opportunities for deriving satisfaction from the nature of the work are available, whatever the language background of the employee. On the other hand, in Finance both the Anglophones and Francophones (few as there are) are excited by the policy-planning and fact-finding that goes on there.

Agriculture appears to be a deviant case; only here does a gap between language groups exist. However, this may be seen to support the thesis about the importance of a departmental ethos.[9] The Francophones are a great deal more isolated from the mainstream of this department than is the case elsewhere. In particular, the Francophone researchers have a somewhat different style of work and do not embrace some of the intellectual concerns which dominate the department and which Francophones consider "English." Thus, the case of Agriculture, rather than devaluing the importance of a "departmental" factor, shows that it can be important in explaining attitudes and behaviour.

C. Variations on the Work-Benefit Theme

A further consideration of those who joined for benefit factors reveals interesting Anglophone-Francophone differences. Anglophone personnel were most likely to state that it was a desire for more security and few job pressures which drew them to the Public Service. This is especially true of those Anglophones whose mother tongue was not English. While 36 per cent of these persons sought security, only 21 per cent of the Anglophones of English mother tongue did so. Many security-seekers had had adverse experiences in private industry or had recently arrived from abroad. The federal Public Service was felt to be a fair employer. Salaries might not be as high as private industry, but raises and promotions (often involving a reclassification of position without change in responsibilities) were regarded as frequent.

Among the Francophones who cited benefit factors, what is striking is the large proportion who admitted that they entered the Public Service mainly because they could not find suitable employment elsewhere and it offered the only job position at the time. More than one in five (22 per cent) of the entire Francophone middle-level entered the Public Service under these extreme circumstances. This makes comprehensible the strong feelings about the benefit aspects of their employment among Francophones. There are, of course, Anglophones who value security, but few—about 9 per cent—who recounted the sort of difficult job-hunting undergone by Francophones.

Francophones at all seniority levels mention the benefits derived from government employment, while it is mainly the Anglophones with long-term service who feel this way (Table 3.2). These Anglophones entered government service in the 1940's and early 1950's, generally with inferior professional or technical training. They are usually grateful that they have been able to go so far despite their lack of education. Here is how a draftsman with 20 years' service and a few technical courses beyond high school phrased his answer:

Round about the end of the war, you're young and you've had big ideas, but then the war ends, and you have to get a job. And there are hundreds of servicemen looking for jobs.

Suddenly, security, whether you like it or not—and even at eighteen things are made more vivid by war—becomes important. You get security-conscious. Put quite bluntly, there was a feeling of large groups of people somehow crawling into security.

The younger Anglophones who have recently joined are much more likely to view the federal administration as an exciting workplace, than are the older generation. Six in ten of the Anglophones with short-term service joined for work reasons. Of course, these younger men are also more likely to have university degrees and to move directly into work areas where individual responsibility and creativity are called for.

TABLE 3.2

Per Cent Joining the Federal Administration for "Benefit" Reasons Among Francophones and Anglophones at the Middle Level of the Canadian Public Service (1965) by Years of Government Service

Francophones		Anglophones	
Years of Service	Per Cent Giving Benefit Reasons	Years of Service	Per Cent Giving Benefit Reasons
5 years or less (N:36)	56	5 years or less (N:60)	30
6 to 14 years (N:63)	51	6 to 14 years (N:73)	41
15 years or more (N:29)	59	15 years or more (N:35)	57
Total (N:128)	55	Total (N:168)	40

The benefits attached to government employment are markedly more important to those from certain geographic areas than from others. On the Anglophone side, it is those raised in Quebec Province (excluding Hull) or the Atlantic Provinces who are most attracted by employment benefits. Among the Francophones, those who grew up in the Capital Region seek

TABLE 3.3

Per Cent Giving Selected Reasons for Joining the Federal Administration Among Francophones and Anglophones at the Middle Level of the Canadian Public Service (1965) by Geographic Origin

Linguistic Group and Geographic Origin	Selected Reasons for Joining					
	Career Opportunities	TOTAL WORK FACTORS	Security	Ottawa-Hull Attraction	Only Job	TOTAL BENEFIT FACTORS
Anglophones						
Ottawa-Hull (N:30)	10	40	23	20	3	47
Quebec (excluding Hull) and the Maritimes (N:24)	29	42	21	4	29	54
Ontario (excluding Ottawa) (N:37)	22	43	35	11	3	49
Western Canada (N:42)	36	62	19	2	12	33
Total (N:168)	23	52	23	8	9	40
Francophones						
Ottawa-Hull (N:55)	9	24	20	24	20	64
Quebec (excluding Hull) (N:47)	26	47	15	2	23	40
Total (N:128)	17	33	19	12	22	55

out benefits more so than their compatriots from the Province of Quebec (excluding Hull) (Table 3.3.). In fact, the Quebec Francophones are remarkably similar to the Anglophones in the reasons they give for entering the government service. Exactly the same percentage—40 per cent—of both *Québecois* and all Anglophones cited benefit factors as their main reason for federal employment. This figure is much lower than that for the Francophone group as a whole (54 per cent) and substantially lower than that of the Francophones from the Ottawa-Hull area (64 per cent). Thus, it is primarily the corps from Ottawa-Hull that makes the Francophone group appear more concerned than the Anglophones about benefit factors. The Ottawa-Hull public servants of French background seem to be jarringly out of tune not only with the Anglophones but also with their fellow Francophones from the Province of Quebec.

It is chiefly those raised in the Ottawa-Hull area who give as their reason for entering the government a desire to be in that region. A fifth of the native Anglophones and nearly a quarter (24 per cent) of the Francophones from the region expressed a wish to be in their "hometown" as their main motive for seeking out a job there. A typical answer:

I guess the main reason that I joined the Civil Service was that in Ottawa where else do you go. The Civil Service was always held up to me as a place of security, the ultimate place for a young man to go after school.

The overall greater preference for Ottawa-Hull among Francophones is not surprising when it is recalled that some 43 per cent of them spent their teenage years in the Ottawa-Hull region.

It is the rare person raised elsewhere in Canada who is specially attracted to the Ottawa-Hull area as a place to work. In particular, few Anglophones from Western Canada or Francophones from Quebec (excluding Hull) ever state that it figures as a main motive for taking up federal employment. For these people it is the character of the work going on there that counts most. This leads into a consideration of those who join for work reasons.

Above all it is the Anglophones from Western Canada and the *Québecois* who are attracted by the work of the government rather than by its benefits. More than six in ten of these Anglophones and 47 per cent of these Francophones mention that the work itself drew them in. The career opportunities offered by government appear to be the major attraction to these persons. By contrast, those from the Ottawa-Hull region, both Anglophones and Francophones, rarely mention that career opportunities played a large part in their reason to join.

It appears, as well, to be those from large cities among both Francophones and Anglophones, who are primarily interested in work factors, more than their fellows from smaller centres (Table 3.4).

TABLE 3.4

Per Cent Joining for Work Reasons Among Francophones and Anglophones at the Middle Level of the Canadian Public Service (1965) by Size of Place of Origin (As of the 1941 Census)

| Size of Place of Origin | Per Cent Joining for Work Reasons | | | |
	Franco- phones	N*	Anglo- phones	N*
Large City 250,000 or More	48	23	59	46
Medium City 50,000-250,000	28	68	48	56
Towns and Rural Areas	35	37	48	60
Total	33	128	52	168

* These are the case bases on which the percentages are calculated.

But it is education which is most clearly the genesis of a concern for creative work. First, we find there is a direct relationship between level of education and joining the government for work reasons (Table 3.5). In both linguistic groups, those with higher university degrees are most likely to be in the federal administration because of the challenging work going on there. Second, it is those with university training in the arts or humanities, rather than science or engineering, and commerce or law, who talk most often of pursuing a government career because of the interesting work (Table 3.6). Those persons with a ''generalist'' education seem to be more desirous of getting a

TABLE 3.5

Per Cent Joining for Work Reasons Among the Francophones and Anglophones at the Middle Level of the Canadian Public Service (1965) by Level of Education

| Level of Education | Per Cent Joining for Work Reasons | | | |
	Franco-phones	N*	Anglo-phones	N*
Some University or Less	22	46	30	44
First University Degree	30	47	48	78
Postgraduate University Degree	54	35	74	46
Total	33	128	52	168

* These are the case bases on which the percentages are calculated.

TABLE 3.6

Per Cent Joining for Work Reasons among Francophones and Anglophones at the Middle Level of the Canadian Public Service (1965) by University Specialization

| University Specialization | Per Cent Joining for Work Reasons | | | |
	Franco-phones	N*	Anglo-phones	N*
Arts and Humanities	57	23	72	32
Science and Engineering	33	40	53	81
Commerce and Law	21	33	44	18
Total	33	128	52	168

* These are the case bases on which the percentages are calculated.

job with intellectual appeal than those with specialist training. This finding somewhat contradicts Marvick's results reported earlier.[10]

After leaving full-time education, the experience of job-changing and switching in one's employment outside the federal administration has a differential impact on the two linguistic groups. Of course, only a small proportion of Francophones had a chaotic work history, but those who had were unlikely to join for work reasons (Table 3.7). The experience of holding a series

TABLE 3.7

Per Cent Joining for Work Reasons Among Francophones and Anglophones at the Middle Level of the Canadian Public Service (1965) by the Nature of Their Work Histories Outside the Federal Administration

Nature of Work History Outside Federal Administration	Per Cent Joining for Work Reasons			
	Franco-phones	N*	Anglo-phones	N*
Direct Entry — No Work History	39	52	45	40
Orderly Work History — No or Few Job Changes	32	60	51	96
Disorderly Work History — A Great Deal of Job-Switching	25	16	56	32
Total	33	128	52	168

* These are the case bases on which the percentages are computed.

of often unrelated jobs, and jobs that sometimes came to an abrupt end, made them yearn after more security. The same experience had the opposite effect on Anglophones. The Anglophones with disorderly work histories are more likely to be attracted by the work itself than are other Anglophones. After switching among jobs and work areas they seem to regard the Public Service as just another employer with an interesting job offer. One reason for the difference between linguistic groups is the scope of the opportunities available to each. For Francophones without a job there is a considerably narrower range of possibilities than there is for Anglophones. The Anglophones have access to the whole of North American industry. In contrast, particularly if they wish to work in French or avoid work settings that are totally English, Francophones must select within a limited framework and their search is made more desperate as a consequence. They need the steady job and income offered by the government; Anglophones know that if the work is not interesting they can easily leave for something else.

There are two further themes that are fairly prominent among those who join for work reasons. First, there are those who find government work attractive because of the unique research or training opportunities it provides. For some of them it is one of the only agencies in the country doing important work in their field; for others it offers training that can be gained nowhere else and which is crucial for a later career in the private sector. The scientists in the Department of Agriculture illustrate one type of careerist who feels this way about federal employment. These men are strongly concerned about scientific accomplishment and gaining recognition in the scientific community. In certain areas of agricultural research, the federal government is the main employer. Here are several representative accounts of the reasons these scientists give for joining the federal service:

At the time (1948-49) the Research Branch of the department (Agriculture) contained at least 95 per cent of the entomologists employed in Canada. It was an exciting time in entomology in the Civil Service then, too. . . . That influenced me away from private industry or teaching. So, I suppose the main reason was that if you wanted to do entomology you automatically went into the Civil Service in those days. It might be different now.

Je n'ai aucun sentiment envers le gouvernement fédéral; c'est pas que j'aime ça ici, la fonction publique. Mais c'est que je peux y faire de la recherche fondamentale.

Well, I don't think it was a case of joining the Civil Service as much as having a chance to work in this lab. It had top people and a top reputation. I have a good opportunity to gain experience in research work, and to build up a reputation of my own. It was the quality of the research that attracted me.

The scientific orientation of these men is strong; their organizational attachment is weak. The guiding theme of their worklives is to do good research and, as it happens, it is the federal government which offers this opportunity. Unlike another type of worker whom I will consider in a moment, they are rarely moved by any sense of "public service" or "national duty."

The federal government offers a special training experience

to others. It appears that a stint in government work is a virtual necessity for moving into certain careers in the private sector. Such is the case, for example, among those who work for private firms that draw up patent applications or law firms that go to court on behalf of businesses involved in a tax suit with the government. Here is how one of these men describes his sojourn in government service:

> Right now I represent the government in tax litigation. Before, while I was with the law firm in Vancouver, I had a good amount of work in this field. I became really interested in it and decided I should get out and see the other side of the operation. I came here for the experience you might say. Most lawyers in this field go through the department (National Revenue) at some time.

Like the research scientists, these men also take a rather opportunistic view of federal employment: as long as they are learning and doing advanced work they will stay on; when it appears that they have picked up enough skills or that their upward career movement has slowed, they will leave. These scientists and professionals, in short, are "discipline-oriented" and "cosmopolitan" in outlook, not firmly tied to a single organization.[11]

Contrast with this, men who sound the second important theme:

> Je voulais venir à Ottawa pour contribuer, via la politique fédérale, au relèvement du niveau de vie et des conditions économiques des Acadiens de l'Ile du Prince-Edouard.

> At university I became interested in social and economic problems. I decided then I wanted to tackle the world's problems by working in the public sector, not for industry. Some professors steered me into economics but an athletic coach was the person who started my interest in community work.

This is not a common motive—it is expressed by only 1 or 2 per cent of Anglophones and Francophones—but it is one that figures importantly in certain work settings that are training grounds for the bureaucratic elite, e.g., Department of Finance, Treasury Board, and the Department of External Affairs. Indeed, this sort of attitude seems to be assumed of those officers whose careers are leading to upper-level positions. Paradoxically, even though such attitudes are assumed, it is often difficult for public servants to be articulate about them. Most felt somewhat modest about voicing what could appear as overly selfless and public-spirited sentiments. Nevertheless, the theme of "public service" is an important part of the ethos of the federal administration, and it especially underlies the efforts of many of its senior personnel.

The foregoing discussion of the "discipline" and "public-service" orientations covers the two themes which are most prominent in the dynamic and creative work settings of the federal administration. One important question remains: Do Anglophones and Francophones equally share these types of attitudes? Rare though they are in these settings, the Francophones appear to be imbued with many of the same feelings. The problem is rather that the federal administration has been able to attract and retain only a few talented Francophones who could work in these areas. Is the absence based on a relative paucity of trained and creative Francophones in the general population or on the refusal of those of real talent to join the federal service? Both factors are probably operative. However, on balance, and especially in recent years, it appears that the refusal to join on the part of Francophones is the more compelling reason. Those who might consider coming know that they must operate within an English cultural ambience. Creative and dynamic as such settings are, due to their unilingual English nature they do not permit the full expression or development of the creative capacity of Francophones.

D. Departmental Selection

To anyone outside of Ottawa, the government is the government. It doesn't break down into departments. I just joined the government. (Information Officer, age 41, with seven years of service and a salary of $11,000.)

Most persons just "drift" into government employment and are not really attracted by a specific department. However, certain departments more than others contain a much smaller proportion of men like these. Such departments are either specifically sought out by persons with particular interests or the departments themselves have evolved mechanisms by which they contact outsiders and bring them in. Often both processes operate in those departments which have few "drifters."

Although I do not have quantified findings, it appears that those with advanced training and specialized interests are most likely to be attracted by a specific department. This has already been suggested by the discussion of the scientists who seek out the Department of Agriculture, the tax lawyers in the Department of National Revenue, and the patent examiners in the Patent Office. Before joining, these men already know many of the specifics of the job they will be in. In the same category would probably fall the natural scientists at the National Research Council, and the social workers and medical personnel at the Department of National Health and Welfare.

A less-focussed but quite definite selection is also made by those who want to get into a department "where the action is." These persons generally divide government departments into two classes—the stuffy, routine ones and the powerful, exciting ones—and they, of course, opt for the latter. The places most commonly chosen are the Departments of Finance, External Affairs, Trade and Commerce, and sometimes the Treasury Board.

I grew up in Manitoba and had no contact with the federal Public Service there. But one summer I worked in Ottawa at D.B.S. (Dominion Bureau of Statistics). That summer for the first time I gained a little bit of a feel for what it was like in Ottawa. . . . Then my specific interests in international affairs and the Far East ruled out D.B.S. and Trade and Commerce. . . . I went to the University of Toronto and learned about the Department of Finance from an Assistant Deputy Minister. His personal influence was an important factor. . . . He told me about Finance being at the centre of things and I've found it to be true.

Some departments are considerably more aggressive than others in going after the type of person they want. The procedures at their disposal range from making available summer employment to university students or faculty, to sending out top officials to the training grounds, up to having a senior person encourage a promising outsider and make special arrangements for his employment. As the last quotation may suggest, it is typically for work settings that regularly need injections of new people with the latest training that the officers are continually searching for able recruits.

There is another but rather special case of government initiative in locating personnel that I will consider at length in a later chapter: what is known among civil servants as the "parachutist." The parachutist drops into the upper levels of the federal administration after developing a career in the private sector or a public service other than the federal one. For these men, special arrangements are made by Cabinet order and they move immediately into a high government post, but not necessarily a powerful one. (Many of these people are appointed to Boards and Commissions and although they draw large salaries they have limited power.) The relative rates at which those of French and English background have gained entry to government circles by this mechanism will be examined. Here, we can anticipate the findings by saying that the slower rate of upward career mobility of Francophones at the middle level means that the parachuting process is used extensively by the government to redress the imbalances at the top which result from the inequalities of the career systems of the departments. Thus Francophones with long experience outside the government are often able to get into the department of their choice by taking advantage of this situation.

E. A Retrospective View of Joining the Public Service

I asked my respondents to look back to the period immediately after they first joined the civil service. How did they feel about the place? Were they committed to staying on and pursuing a career? Of course, their views about the past may be inaccurate, flavoured as they are by their present feelings. This is not important. I am chiefly interested in the ways Francophones and Anglophones react to their work environment. Answers to these questions reveal something of such differences and similarities between the linguistic groups.

Nearly equal proportions—31 per cent of Francophones and 32 per cent of Anglophones—report that their initial feeling was one of firm commitment, that they liked the work and the thought of moving elsewhere never crossed their minds (Table 3.8). Turning to the uncommitted, we find the Francophones slightly but not significantly more prevalent here—50 per cent of Francophones and 44 per cent of Anglophones state that they were uncommitted at the time of joining. The interesting finding is the differing distribution of the linguistic groups within the uncommitted category. The Francophones are more likely to claim that they had definite plans for leaving while the Anglophones assert they were just indifferent. In short, the Francophones were considerably more likely than the Anglophones to consider abandoning a career in the federal administration soon after it began. This difference is a substantial one; it holds up within the several career types and seniority groups of the study.

It appears that at the outset of their careers professional and scientific personnel in both linguistic groups are especially likely to be uncommitted to government work (Table 3.9). Here is how a young economist expresses this feeling. He has been in the government for just over a year:

> I planned on staying about two years when I joined. I am thinking now about going back to university. But if I am listened to and find I can get my ideas put into force, I may stay on. Right now I hold a wait-and-see attitude.

Two accountants in the early stages of their government careers show the intentions to quit that are more prevalent among the Francophones.

> Non, je n'étais pas déterminé à rester; je voulais quitter éventuellement pour quelque chose de plus intéressant comme travail.

Au début je n'avais pas l'intention de demeurer. Je voulais prendre de l'expérience, compléter mes études par les soirs et possiblement quitter par la suite pour un bureau de comptables ou pour l'entreprise privée.

Thus the Francophones, particularly the highly-trained professionals and scientists, enter the federal administration in a more tentative manner than the Anglophones. As we will see in the following chapters, the wisdom of making only a tentative commitment is often verified when they discover the language and career disadvantages they have to overcome.

TABLE 3.8

Degree of Commitment to Staying in the Public Service at the Time of Entry Among Francophones and Anglophones at the Middle Level of the Canadian Public Service (1965)

Degree of Commitment at the Time of Entry	Franco-phones		Anglo-phones	
Firmly Committed — felt they would definitely stay	31		32	
Mildly Committed — did not mind the work and would stay if promotions came	3		6	
TOTAL COMMITTED		34		38
Indifferent — did not feel at all committed	23		35	
Leaving — were determined to leave after a definite period	27		9	
TOTAL UNCOMMITTED		50		44
Undecided — no strong feelings were going to wait and see	13		14	
Other or Not Determined	3		5	
TOTAL	100 (N:128)		101 (N:168)	

TABLE 3.9

Per Cent Expressing Lack of Commitment to Staying in the Public Service at the Time of Entry Among Francophones and Anglophones at the Middle Level of the Canadian Public Service (1965) by Career Type

Career Type	Francophones				Anglophones			
	In-different	Leaving	Total Un-committed	N*	In-different	Leaving	Total Un-committed	N*
Professional and Scientific	30	23	53	43	37	8	45	84
Administrative	19	29	48	31	33	10	43	42
Technical and Semi-Professional	19	28	47	54	24	14	38	42
Total	23	27	50	128	35	9	44	168

* These are the case bases on which the percentages are computed.

F. General Conclusions

I have now further specified the relative influence of ethnic-linguistic, career, regional, and organization cultures.

General confirmation was provided for Hypothesis 2. Francophones more than Anglophones were concerned about organizational benefits. This applied within various career types. However, the extent of concern for work or benefit factors varied considerably *between* career types. Scientists and policy-makers placed most emphasis on work factors, followed by semi-professionals, engineers, technicians and lower administrators. Occupational (career) culture, therefore, produced marked and patterned differences in concern for work or benefit aspects of a federal post, but ethnic-linguistic culture blunted the influence of career culture. Francophones were prone to put more weight on benefit factors than were Anglophones.

However, some findings contradicted Hypothesis 2. *Québecois* were similar to the Anglophones in the prevalence of concern about work factors. Among the Anglophones there is also the suggestion that those of non-English mother tongue —largely persons from minority cultures—are especially likely to value benefit factors.

Departmental culture also produces patterned variation. The routine, service organizations are havens for the benefit-minded, while persons joining research and policy settings state they were attracted to the work going on there.

The picture, in short, is a complicated one. Career and organizational cultures seem to select out unequal proportions of persons concerned about work or benefit factors. Francophones however, and especially those from the Ottawa-Hull region, are more prone than Anglophones to be in search of security.

Notes

[1]Dwaine Marvick, *Career Perspectives in a Bureaucratic Setting* (Ann Arbor, 1954).
[2]Frederick Herzberg, *et al.*, *Job Attitudes: Review of Research and Opinion* (Pittsburgh, 1957).
[3]Frederick Herzberg, *et. al.*, *The Motivation to Work* (New York, 1959).

⁴*Ibid.*, p. 113.

⁵Lyman W. Porter, "Job Attitudes in Management: I. Perceived Deficiencies in Need Fulfillment as a Function of Job Level," *Journal of Applied Psychology*, 46 (December, 1962), pp. 375-84.

⁶Frank Friedlander and Eugene Walton, "Positive and Negative Motivations Toward Work," *Administrative Science Quarterly*, 9 (September, 1964), pp. 194-207.

⁷Robert Blauner, *Alienation and Freedom, The Factory Worker and His Industry* (Chicago, 1964).

⁸Frank Friedlander, "Comparative Work Value Systems," *Personnel Psychology*, 18 (Spring, 1965), pp. 1-20.

⁹The examination of a "deviant case" to aid in clarifying a general explanation of the relationship between factors is a usual procedure in sociological analysis. The leading example of this technique is the clarification of Michels' "iron law of oligarchy" derived from a study of a democratic trade union. See Seymour Martin Lipset, *et al.*, *Union Democracy* (Glencoe, Ill., 1956).

¹⁰That these "generalists," or "institutionalists" to use Marvick's term, are more interested in work factors may be a by-product of the fact that many of the Canadian generalists were doing exciting policy and personnel work while Marvick's institutionalists seemed to be chiefly routine administrators and career-minded military men.

¹¹The distinction between "cosmopolitans" and "locals" or "organizationals" derives from Alvin W. Gouldner, "Cosmopolitans and Locals: Towards an Analysis of Latent Social Roles—I, II," *Administrative Science Quarterly*, 2 (December, 1957), pp. 281-306; (March, 1958), pp. 444-80. A similar distinction is developed in a study of staff experts in labor unions, Harold L. Wilensky, *Intellectuals in Labour Unions: Organizational Pressures on Professional Roles* (Glencoe, Ill., 1956), Part III.

Chapter Four
Bureaucratic Careers

A career is a standardized and socially recognized sequence of related work roles within an occupational community (e.g., law, printing) or work organization (e.g., factory, federal department) or through several occupations or organizations.[1] Careers are standard routes in that many persons have followed the same sequence. The movement from position to position has become patterned and regular. Careers are socially recognized in that the sequence is known to many segments of the population and has acquired a public identity. A career, therefore, is a sequence of related work roles, a sequence that is regularly repeated and publicly acknowledged.

That a career involves a sequence of *related roles* means that each role is an outgrowth of the preceding role and, in turn, shapes the nature of subsequent moves. The work roles which compose a career "feed into" one another. Career movement is a natural flow. Such patterned sequences, of course, take many forms. One of these is the bureaucratic career: entry at or near the bottom of a bureaucracy and advancement from one post to a higher one as the person acquires skill or seniority. In the process one might forsake one occupation and begin another. A second form of career, that of the model or prostitute for example, involves ascent soon after entry to the field followed by a decline with increasing age and deterioration of physique. Professional athletes take longer to climb to the top but their later years also involve a career in decline. A third form of career involves vertical movement like the bureaucratic career, but the person remains a solo performer working on his own. Many who provide expert service—lawyers, medical doctors, repairmen and other craftsmen—are likely to have careers like this. Other expert servers might begin solo but either join or create an organization. Yet another (a fourth) form of career carries persons from one organization to another of the same sort, but at much the same level. Examples are nurses and high school teachers. A variant of this form involves movement between organizations that differ in function. Tax lawyers who go from federal service into private firms demonstrate this pattern. The main point, however, is that the bureaucratic career has to be seen as one of several distinct models.

The concept of the bureaucratic career provides a means of examining the work histories of federal employees during their years of government employment. It directs one to ask the following question: How quickly and by what processes do people move upward along the departmental career routes?

A. The Bureaucratic Career

A bureaucratic organization is an enduring social system composed of (1) officials occupying posts that are linked together in a hierarchy of authority and communication, i.e., most officials supervise others and, in turn, are supervised by superiors, (2) files and records which are maintained and regularly updated by clerks, and (3) a complete set of formal rules and procedures which specify what each official or clerk is to do and how or when they can gain promotions.[2] This form of social organization has two by-products that are especially relevant to my discussion: the availability of careers that can encompass one's complete worklife and the rational deployment of personnel in pursuit of organizational goals.

The bureaucratic career is one of regular movement upwards along the established paths in a bureaucracy on the basis of a combination of competent performance, acquired skill or education, practical experience, or seniority. The important feature of bureaucracies is that upward movement should depend on technical competence and able performance. In the federal administration this view is enshrined in the merit system which replaced patronage and based appointments and promotions on "open competitions" in which the post went to the candidate with the most points in his favour.

The availability of bureaucratic careers involving regular promotions for those of ability has important consequences for both persons and their society. An orderly career that offers the prospects of both prestige and advancement encourages persons to acquire the necessary training or education and to strive for excellence in performance. Conventions and standards of behaviour develop among those in the career; deviation is discouraged. In this way, careers supply meaning and direction to individual life.[3] In the society at large, bureaucratic careers contribute to the levelling of social differences. Since competence, not kin ties, political contacts, race, or ethnicity is the deciding factor, persons of ability from all social levels and backgrounds are *eligible* to begin these careers. Lack of access to the necessary education does of course tend to eliminate certain categories of persons but, if equality of educational opportunity were available, these careers would be open to anyone of ability. Max Weber has commented on this process:

> The development of bureaucracy greatly favors the levelling of social classes and this can be shown historically to be the normal tendency. Conversely, every process of social levelling creates a favourable situation for the development of bureaucracy; for it tends to eliminate class privileges, which include the appropriation of authority as well as the occupation of offices on an honorary basis or as an avocation by virtue of wealth. This combination everywhere inevitably foreshadows the development of mass democracy. . . .[4]

For both person and society bureaucratic careers open opportunities for all those who have skill and a will to work and, conversely, make it more difficult to inherit a social position.

Despite the emphasis on ability as the key factor in gaining entry and promotions, the views of sociological theorists of bureaucracy and the rhetoric of bureaucrats contain a mixed emphasis. Weber, for example, reveals this ambiguity in his description of a bureaucrat's career:

> He moves from the lower, less important, and lower paid to the higher positions. The average official naturally desires a mechanical fixing of the conditions of promotions: if not of the offices, at least of the salary levels. He wants these conditions fixed in terms of "seniority," or possibly according to grades achieved in a developed system of expert examinations.[5]

Elsewhere, Weber writes, "There is a system of 'promotion' according to seniority or to achievement, or both."[6] But which of the two is primary?

The same theme appears in the interviews I held with middle-level men in bureaucratic organizations. The following are the comments of two professional men, the first an engineer, the second an economist.

> Many times they promote the wrong man—the guy sitting on his ass with seniority. The capable young men leave.

> I don't think our superiors want "yes" men. They want new ideas and they want them pushed as long as they are good.

In addition to seniority and expertise, students of organizations and employees alike often note the place of "informal factors in career achievement."[7] When men similar in age and education are competing for promotion, their social backgrounds and social assets may become deciding factors. Dalton, for instance, found that ethnicity, religion, participation in a certain sporting club, political affiliation, and membership in the Masons were all taken account of among the salaried managers in the factory he studied. Junior managers in their "search for mobility ladders sharpened their sensitivity to the attitudes and attributes of superiors and induced competition to please."[8] For their part, the senior managers often invoked the same unofficial criteria in making promotional decisions. For, as E. C. Hughes tells us in his study of an English-dominated factory in French Canada, awarding a promotion is a "vote of confidence."[9] "In general, there is probably a strong bias in favor of appointing for higher positions a man of the kind liked and trusted by the appointing group."[10]

Our interest here, then, is in social mobility: the extent and relative speeds of movement upwards in economic rank through these bureaucratic careers.[11] As a corollary, I will be interested in assessing the influence of expertise, as indicated by level and type of education, on salary attainment. Or, to be more exact, I will try to determine the influence of expertise as compared to such factors as class origins, age, and seniority.

In social research concerning changes in economic status,

several approaches are possible. Many studies concentrate on intergenerational mobility: a comparison of some aspect of the economic level of a person with the level attained by the person's father or family of origin. Wilensky argues that to date such measures have contained gross errors and he doubts "if anything can be said with confidence about rates of intergenerational mobility and their trend."[12] In addition, on theoretical grounds, the second main type of social mobility, career movement within one's lifetime, seems to exert a stronger influence on feelings and behavior than intergenerational mobility, except at one point in life. Persons early in their career are very conscious of where they stand in relation to their parents. Later in life, "the important comparisons are made with their own pasts; and consequent interpretations of success or failure are made in the context of contemporary reference groups."[13] Since my focus is on relatively young persons at mid-career it seems appropriate to adopt both approaches. I will first see how the two language groups have fared in relation to their parents. Then I will consider the worklife mobility of Anglophones and Francophones.

B. Intergenerational Mobility

Comparisons of their own position with their familial departure point continue to be important for these careerists. As well, it is possible to see whether Weber's comments on the levelling of social differences have much relevance when we compare their attainment to their fathers'. Have many managed to use a bureaucratic career to rise above their parents? Has there been much inheritance of social level or have some people even started at a lower level?

At the outset, it should be noted that we have adjusted the comparison to remove some unfairness. To pit a young person against the attainment of his middle-aged father seems harsher than to compare an older man with his father's attainment. Therefore, we use different standards for younger and older careerists in determining the nature of their intergenerational movement. Table 4.1 shows how the person's class origins (as determined by father's salary, occupation, education, when the respondent was in his teens—see Chapter 2 or Appendix 2 for the exact coding of class origins), and current age and salary level have been combined to provide a mobility measure. For instance, those of lower-middle class origins who are quite young (25-35 years) but earning a relatively large salary (over $8,000 a year in 1965), are classed as having high upward mobility. On the other extreme, persons whose familial point of departure into the work world was the upper-middle class but who are now earning under $8,000 a year are considered as experiencing high downward movement.

TABLE 4.1

Amount of Intergenerational Mobility as Determined by Class Origin, Current Age, and Current Salary Among Those at the Middle Level of the Canadian Public Service (1965)

Amount of Intergenerational Mobility	Measurement Components		
	Class Origin	Current Age	Current Salary
High Upward	Lower Middle	25-35	$8,000+
	Working	25-35	$7-8,000
	Working	25-45	$8,000+
	Farm	25-35	$7-8,000
	Farm	25-45	$8,000+
Slight Upward	Upper Middle	25-45	$12,000+
	Lower Middle	36-45	$8,000+
	Working	25-45	under $7,000
	Working	36-45	$7-9,000
	Farm	25-45	under $7,000
	Farm	36-45	$7-8,000
None	Upper Middle	25-35	$8-9,000
	Upper Middle	25-45	$9-12,000
	Lower Middle	25-35	under $8,000
Slight Downward	Lower Middle	36-45	under $8,000
High Downward	Upper Middle	25-45	under $8,000
	Upper Middle	36-45	$8-9,000

Earlier I indicated that nearly half the Francophones (49 per cent) and 44 per cent of the Anglophones at the middle level were of working class or farm origins. Since they are now in careers of a "white collar" or middle class sort, this is one indication of upward movement for a considerable number of persons. Thus, it should not surprise us to find that the federal administration is an important avenue of upward mobility for equally large segments of both the Francophone and Anglophone group: just over 60 per cent of the persons in both linguistic groups have attained a higher position than their family of origin through government employment (Table 4.2). A sizeable proportion in each group (20 per cent of Francophones, 17 per cent of Anglophones) have at least maintained the same level. On the other hand, in this era of expanding economic opportunities and a growing GNP in Canada, we find that about a fifth in both language groups are below the level of their parents. Many of these, of course, may surpass their parents by the end of their careers. But the significant finding is that for the majority of middle-level men from both language groups, to work for the federal government has meant to improve one's lot, financially at least, in comparison to one's parents.

TABLE 4.2

Amount of Intergenerational Mobility of Francophones and Anglophones at the Middle Level of the Canadian Public Service (1965)

Linguistic Group	Amount of Intergenerational Mobility					
	High Down-ward	Slight Down-ward	None	Slight Upward	High Upward	Total
Francophones (N:128)	10	8	20	27	35	100
Anglophones (N:168)	12	9	17	29	33	100

In both language groups, the professionals and scientists have the highest proportion showing a marked improvement (Table 4.3). Over 45 per cent of them have experienced high upward mobility. However, when upward mobility of any sort (i.e., slight plus high upward) is considered it is the administrators in both language groups who have raised their station in life compared with their parents. Slightly more than two-thirds (68

TABLE 4.3

Amount of Intergenerational Mobility of Francophones and Anglophones at the Middle Level of the Canadian Public Service (1965) by Career Type

Linguistic Group and Career Type	Amount of Intergenerational Mobility					
	High Downward	Slight Downward	None	Slight Upward	High Upward	Total
Francophones						
Professional and Scientific (N:43)	16	5	23	7	49	100
Technical and Semi-professional	9	13	15	35	28	100
Administrative (N:31)	3	3	26	38	29	99
Anglophones						
Professional and Scientific (N:84)	12	5	20	17	46	100
Technical and Semi-professional (N:42)	19	12	17	36	17	101
Administrative (N:42)	7	12	12	41	29	101

TABLE 4.4

Educational Attainment of Francophones and Anglophones at the Middle Level of the Canadian Public Service (1965) Compared to the Attainment of Their Fathers

Linguistic Group	Education of Official Compared to Father					
	Less Education	Same Level	Slightly Higher	Markedly Higher	Not Indicated	Total
Francophones (N:128)	2	10	21	64	2	99
Anglophones (N:168)	5	13	27	53	2	100

per cent) of Francophone administrators and 69 per cent of Anglophone administrators have experienced upward mobility. On the other extreme are members of the Anglophone technical and semi-professional staff. Only 17 per cent of them have experienced high upward mobility, although overall a sizeable proportion (52 per cent) have undergone some upward movement.

A major factor accounting for the relative success of these careerists is that they are significantly better educated than their parents. I compare the educational attainment of the government employees with the attainment of their fathers in Table 4.4. Few had less education or the same educational attainment as their fathers. The majority—64 per cent of Francophones and 53 per cent of Anglophones—have a markedly higher level of training. Note that it is the Francophones who show the most substantial improvement in education. This confirms the notion that since the Second World War there has been a quickened growth of educational opportunities in French Canada.

The fact that high upward movement is most probable among professionals and scientists is partially explained by the finding that this group shows the most marked educational improvement compared to their fathers (Table 4.5). As well, the lack of high upward movement for Anglophone technical and semi-professional persons reflects, in part, the fact that this group has not made substantial educational improvements over the previous generation. In fact, 14 per cent of them have *less* education than what their fathers obtained.

The preponderance of technical and semi-professional staff in National Revenue accounts for that department displaying relatively low rates of upward mobility for Francophones as well as Anglophones (Table 4.6). On the other hand, Anglophones in Finance and Francophones in Agriculture—both groups where professionals, scientists, or administrators are numerous —show comparatively high rates of upward progress for personnel. The other departments stand between these extremes.

Our general finding, therefore, is that the current generation of middle-level men at mid-career has made significant financial advances over the position of its families of origin. The pattern of intergenerational mobility is similar for Anglophones and Francophones. The critical factor appears to be education:

TABLE 4.5

Educational Attainment of Francophones and Anglophones at the Middle Level of the Canadian Public Service (1965) Compared to the Attainment of Their Fathers by Career Type

Linguistic Group and Career Type	Education of Official Compared to Father					
	Less Education	Same Level	Slightly Higher	Markedly Higher	Not Indicated	Total
Franco-phones						
Professional and Scientific (N:43)	2	9	14	72	2	99
Technical and Semi-professional (N:54)	4	7	24	65	—	100
Administrative (N:31)	0	16	26	52	7	101
Anglo-phones						
Professional and Scientific (N:84)	2	12	14	70	1	99
Technical and Semi-professional (N:42)	14	14	38	29	5	100
Administrative (N:42)	2	14	33	50	0	99

TABLE 4.6

Per Cent with High Upward Mobility Among Francophones and Anglophones at the Middle Level of the Canadian Public Service (1965) by Department

Department	Francophones		Anglophones	
	Per Cent With High Upward	N*	Per Cent With High Upward	N*
State	36	33	37	38
Finance	—	6	43	28
Agriculture	43	28	35	37
Public Works	39	28	31	32
National Revenue	24	33	27	33
Total	35	128	33	168

* This is the case base on which the percentage is computed.

where persons obtain more education than their parents they are also likely to obtain posts of greater pay and prestige.

C. Career Mobility

Do the Anglophones and Francophones move up the departmental career routes at much the same rate and go the same distance? Are there disparities between persons of a similar age, seniority, and educational level in the same career, but from different language groups? The findings here concern the amount of "success," as measured in salary terms, enjoyed by persons of different linguistic origins in the federal administration.

At the outset two facts about the worklife of Francophones in the Public Service must be noted:

(1) For a large segment, as we have seen in Chapter 2, employment in the federal Public Service was their first permanent job. This is the case for 41 per cent of Francophones at the middle level. The comparable figure for Anglophones is 24 per cent.

(2) In terms of years of federal service, the proportion of

Francophones with long service is as great as that of the Anglophones (Table 4.7). Twenty-three per cent of Francophones and 24 per cent of Anglophones have served for 15 years or more.

TABLE 4.7

Years of Service in the Federal Administration of Francophones and Anglophones at the Middle Level of the Canadian Public Service (1965)

Linguistic Group	Years of Service			
	1-5	6-14	15 and Up	Total
Francophones (N:128)	28	49	23	100
Anglophones (N:168)	33	44	24	101

These findings indicate that although the Francophones tend to enter government work much earlier in their worklife than Anglophones, they do not stay. With their headstart in federal employment, it would be expected that they would have a longer average tenure than Anglophones. This is not the case. Although Anglophones enter later in their worklife, an apparent early "fall-out" from the ranks of the Francophones permits them to catch up. This is clearly seen in age distribution. At the middle level relatively fewer Francophones are in the older 41-45 age group (Table 4.8). Thus, for a variety of reasons, many of the early-joining Francophones choose not to make federal service a lifetime career despite its initial attraction.

TABLE 4.8

Age Level of Francophones and Anglophones at the Middle Level of the Canadian Public Service (1965)

Linguistic Group	Age in Years				
	25-30	31-35	36-40	41-45	Total
Francophones (N:128)	13	28	30	30	101
Anglophones (N:168)	13	17	32	39	101

Since middle-level Anglophones tend to be concentrated in the older age groups and middle-level Francophones in the younger age groups, it will be important to hold age constant in making comparisons of salary attainment. As well, it will be necessary to make comparisons within the same career types or educational levels. For Francophones are concentrated in technical and semi-professional and administrative careers while Anglophones are over-represented in professional and scientific ones (Figure 4.1). Technicians, semi-professionals, and administrators usually have lower pay and prestige than professionals and scientists. In general they are either directly serving professionals or scientists, or in some way facilitating their work. This means that in most work settings Francophones are involved in duties more peripheral to the main goals of the department than are Anglophones.

At the middle level the distribution of Francophones varies markedly both between departments and within careers in a single department. It will be recalled that 920 persons fell within the established age and salary brackets in the five departments (see Table 1.1). On one extreme, the personnel of the Departments of Agriculture and Finance are only 9 and 11 per cent Francophone respectively at the middle level. Public Works with 14 per cent and National Revenue (Taxation Division) with 18 per cent Francophones hold the middle ground. On the other extreme, Secretary of State has a third of its middle-level personnel designated as Francophones. However, the Francophones in Secretary of State are located largely in one sector, not randomly distributed throughout the department. In the Translation Bureau they compose 82 per cent of the middle-level employees. That part of Secretary of State including the Patent Office is only 12 per cent Francophone. In short, while Finance, Agriculture, and the Patent Office are largely Anglophone preserves, Francophones dominate the Translation Bureau.

Moreover, in Public Works 42 per cent of the Anglophone population at the middle-level are professionals (either engineers or architects), compared to 32 per cent of the Francophones. The professionals execute the main functions of the department and here Anglophones have the edge. Similarly, in National Revenue, 27 per cent of the Francophones but 36 per cent of the Anglophones are qualified Assessors (chartered accountants). Finally, in Agriculture, Francophones tend to be found in lower-administration or in providing veterinary inspection services. While the majority (52 per cent) of Anglophones are researchers, only 43 per cent of Francophones are involved in the department's main research activities. These data suggest that, at the middle level, Francophones not only are concentrated in lower-powered units providing services to the rest of the federal administration (Translation Bureau) or the public (National Revenue, Public Works) but also they are less likely to be in those careers which are at the vital centre of their departments. Clearly, therefore, it will be imperative to hold constant not only age but also career types.

FIGURE 4.1

Career Types of Francophones and Anglophones at the Middle Level of the Canadian Public Service (1965)

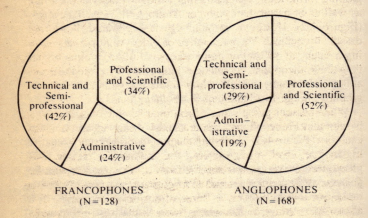

FRANCOPHONES
(N = 128)

ANGLOPHONES
(N = 168)

Analysis by Cross-Tabulations

Given the facts in the previous paragraphs, it is not too surprising to find that a considerably larger proportion of Anglophones than Francophones are earning high salaries (Table

4.9). But this is not my main concern. The emphasis of this section is on comparisons within age groups, educational levels, and career types.

TABLE 4.9

Salary Level of Francophones and Anglophones at the Middle Level of the Canadian Public Service (1965)

Linguistic Group	Salary Per Annum			
	$6200-$7999	$8000-$9999	$10000 or More	Total
Francophones (N:128)	48	43	9	100
Anglophones (N:168)	43	31	26	100

Figures 4.2, 4.3, and 4.4 present the general findings in graphic form. First, it appears that younger Francophones fare as well as or better than younger Anglophones in salary terms (Figure 4.2). However, at older age levels Francophones are drastically behind. The percentage of older Anglophones earning a salary of $9,000 or more a year is fully 37 points higher than the Francophone percentage. Interestingly, while the probability of earning a high salary increases with age for Anglophones, age is a handicap for Francophones.

When persons at the same educational level are compared, it is seen that Francophones are at a salary disadvantage in every category (Figure 4.3). Although the proposition pertains that the higher the level of education, the higher the salary, Anglophones derive greater benefit from it. The gap between the per cent of Francophones and of Anglophones earning $9,000 or more per annum widens as level of education increases. It is about 9 percentage points among those with no university training, but increases to 20 points among employees with post-graduate degrees.

The story is similar for Francophones in the same career fields as Anglophones: a smaller percentage in each field earn high salaries (Figure 4.4). The gap is smallest in administrative careers, but in professional and scientific fields Francophones are nearly 20 points lower than the Anglophones.

FIGURE 4.2

Percentage of Francophones and Anglophones at the Middle Level of the Canadian Public Service (1965) Earning $9,000 or More Per Annum by Age Level

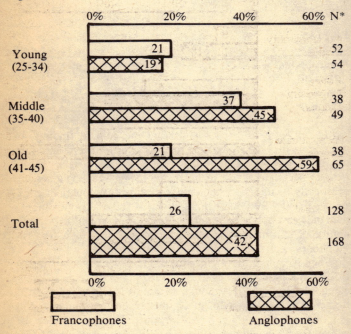

Age Level	*Percentage Earning $9,000 or More Per Annum*	N*
Young (25-34)	21 / 19	52 / 54
Middle (35-40)	37 / 45	38 / 49
Old (41-45)	21 / 59	38 / 65
Total	26 / 42	128 / 168

Francophones   Anglophones

* The figures in this column represent the total number of cases found at each age level. This figure provides the base on which the per cent earning $9,000 or more per annum is calculated.

FIGURE 4.3

Percentage of Francophones and Anglophones at the Middle Level of the Canadian Public Service (1965) Earning $9,000 or More Per Annum by Educational Level

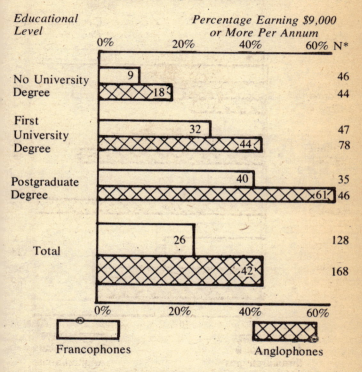

* The figures in this column represent the total number of cases found at each educational level. This figure provides the base on which the per cent earning $9,000 or more per annum is calculated.

FIGURE 4.4

Percentage of Francophones and Anglophones at the Middle Level of the Canadian Public Service (1965) Earning $9,000 or More Per Annum by Career Type

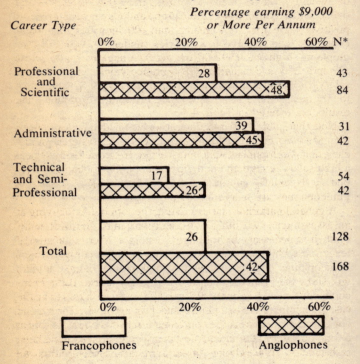

* The figures in this column represent the total number of cases found in each career type. This figure provides the base on which the per cent earning $9,000 or more per annum is calculated.

The foregoing can be briefly summarized in statistical terms by the use of Somers' "d."[14] This measure assesses percentage differences, as in the present case, where a dichotomous independent variable, linguistic group, is related to a dichotomous dependent variable, salary level (under $9,000 or $9,000 and over), within various age, education, and career categories. A positive value for "d" greater than .00 indicates that Francophones tend to have low salaries (under $9,000) and Anglophones high ones ($9,000 and over). A negative value below .00 indicates a concentration of Francophones in the higher salary levels and Anglophones in the lower levels. A value close to .00 means there is no difference in linguistic groups. The results are offered in Table 4.10.

Note that Table 4.10 introduces two factors that have not been treated so far. First, concerning years of service (seniority), it is clear that Anglophones with long service are more likely to be at a high salary level than are their Francophone colleagues. Second, it is chiefly in the "Arts and Humanities" field that Francophones are markedly off the Anglophone pace.

A general pattern is starting to emerge, but before arriving at an assessment, two other considerations must be dealt with. First, it is necessary to hold age constant at every educational level and within each career type. Obviously, a comparison of Francophone degree-holders to Anglophone degree-holders will show the Francophones at lower salary levels, if the Francophones tend to be younger. Since I know this is likely to be the case, it is imperative to enter a control for age level. The second consideration is to treat the combined effect of several factors at a time on salary attainment. So far my comparisons have been restricted to Francophone-Anglophone differences within one or two categories (age group, career type, educational level and age group, and so on). A more complex, yet more realistic, picture can be drawn if the combined effect of age, seniority, education, and career type on salary level can be stated. It then becomes possible to pinpoint those combinations of traits that bring Anglophones decidedly higher salaries than Francophones. This exercise requires the use of multiple-regression techniques; it will be conducted in the next section.

Now let us carve each educational level into two age groups (Table 4.11). It appears that young Francophones do as well or

TABLE 4.10

Summary of the Relationships Between Ethnolinguistic Affinity and Salary Attainment Controlling for Selected Factors Among Middle Level Employees in the Canadian Public Service (1965)

Selected Factors	Strength of Relationship (Somers' "d")	Case Base Franco-phones	Case Base Anglo-phones
Age			
25-34 Years	—.041	52	54
35-40 Years	.082	38	49
41-45 Years	.352	38	65
Length of Federal Employment			
5 Years or Less	.237	36	60
6-15 Years	.096	64	65
16 Years or More	.337	28	33
Education			
Some University or Less	.205	46	44
First University Degree	.115	47	78
Postgraduate Degree	.205	35	46
Educational Specialization			
Arts and Humanities	.333	23	32
Science and Engineering	.162	40	81
Commerce and Law	.098	32	18
Career Type			
Professional — Scientific	.183	43	84
Technical — Semi-Professional	.142	54	42
Administrative	.065	31	42

* When a dichotomous independent variable (linguistic group: Francophones or Anglophones) is related to a dichotomous dependent variable (salary level: Under $9000 or $9000 or more), Somers' "d" serves as a summary measure of percentage differences. It identifies the extent to which the cases are clustered in the upper-left and lower-right cells, or the lower-left and upper-right cells. In the present case, a positive value greater than .00 indicates that Francophones tend to have low salaries and Anglophones high ones. A negative value below .00 indicates a concentration of Francophones in the higher salary levels and Anglophones in the lower levels. A value close to .00 reveals that there is no difference between linguistic groups in their salary distributions. The statistic is fully discussed in Robert H. Somers, "A New Asymmetric Measure of Association for Ordinal Variables," *American Sociological Review,* 27 (December 1962), pp. 799-811.

better than young Anglophones: among those without university degrees they do as well; at the graduate and postgraduate levels, young Francophones do better. It is among older employees at all levels of training that Francophones find themselves in an inferior position. In particular, the Francophone-Anglophone gap for older university graduates is quite dramatic. Francophones are somewhat behind the Anglophones with first university degrees but are considerably behind at the postgraduate level. Although younger Francophones and Anglophones now start as equals, older Francophones are significantly behind their Anglophone equivalents.

Age is again a critical factor in each career type (Table 4.11): young Francophones do as well as their Anglophone colleagues but older Anglophones have moved farther up the salary scale than Francophones of the same age in the same careers. In fact, young Francophones in scientific-professional posts do better, and those in administrative posts do considerably better than their Anglophone counterparts. In both these fields the situation is reversed in the older age group: Anglophones are considerably ahead of Francophones in professional-scientific and administrative careers. Again, it is the older Francophones who find that they are on unequal terms with their Anglophone peers.

I now turn to regression analysis which will permit the treatment of the simultaneous effect of several factors on salary attainment. It also allows for a more refined breakdown of factors than has been possible up to this point.

Analysis by Multiple Regression[15]

I postulate that salary level (S) in these federal organizations is a function of the following variables: age (A), education (E), career type (CT), years of service (YS), ethnolinguistic affinity (L), and a random component (U). This general relationship is represented as follows:

$$S = f(A, E, CT, YS, L, U) \qquad (1)$$

If one postulates that total salary can reasonably be viewed as the result of the above factors working in essentially an additive

TABLE 4.11

Summary of the Relationships Between Ethnolinguistic Affinity and Salary Attainment Controlling for Selected Factors Among Middle Level Employees in the Canadian Public Service (1965)

Selected Factors	Strength of Relationship (Somers' "d")*	Case Base	
		Franco-phones	Anglo-phones
Education and Age			
Some University or Less 25-36 Years	.00	16	16
Some University or Less 37-45 Years	.219	30	28
First University Degree 25-36 Years	−.131	28	32
First University Degree 37-45 Years	.224	19	46
Postgraduate Degree 25-36 Years	−.033	22	21
Postgraduate Degree 37-45 Years	.414	13	25
Career Type and Age			
Professional — Scientific 25-36 Years	−.050	27	37
Professional — Scientific 37-45 Years	.263	16	47
Technical — Semi-Professional 25-36 Years	.035	24	16
Technical — Semi-Professional 37-45 Years	.197	30	26
Administrative 25-36 Years	−.226	15	16
Administrative 37-45 Years	.278	16	26

* See footnote to Table 4.10.

fashion (i.e., that there are few or no interaction effects among the explanatory variables), then relationship (1) may be rewritten:

$$S = B_0 + B_1A + B_2E + B_3CT + B_4YS + B_5L + U \qquad (2)$$

In (2) the B's are partial correlation coefficients; each measures the effect on the dependent variable, S, of a unit change in the independent variable. Thus, for example, if one estimates the age variable, B_1 to be $50, one would then predict that a man 40 years of age would earn $50 more per year than a man having the same characteristics, but only 39 years old.

This approach accommodates continuous variables like salary level, age, and years of service, but is not directly applicable to variables like career type or ethnolinguistic affinity which contain discrete categories. To handle the latter variables, I treated them as binary or "dummy" variables,[16] a technique which also permitted more refined breakdowns. Concerning ethnolinguistic affinity, I split the Francophone and Anglophone groups into unilingual and bilingual sectors. This involved using the response to a question in which Francophones rated their ability in English and Anglophones their ability in French. Self-ratings are, of course, not valid measures of actual linguistic competence, but they do allow us to see in gross terms whether those who feel confident in their use of a second language differ from those who feel able to work well in only one language. This operation concerning ethnolinguistic affinity produced four categories rather than the usual two.

Ethnolinguistic Affinity

FR-U	Unilingual Francophones
FR-B	Bilingual Francophones
ANG-B	Bilingual Anglophones
ANG-U	Unilingual Anglophones

Concerning education, I redefined the university-degree level to distinguish between "Arts" and "Science-Engineering" streams. This is the revised variable:

Education Level

E1   Secondary school completed or less

E2   Some University Training, but no degree, or some technical training beyond completed Secondary School

E3   First University Degree: a degree, usually a Bachelors in Arts, Commerce, or Social Science

E4   First University Degree: a degree, usually a Bachelors in Science, Engineering, Applied Science, Forestry, Math, or Architecture

E5   Postgraduate Degree: a degree, usually either a Masters or Doctors in Arts, Social Science, Philosophy, or a Law degree (LL.B.)

E6   Postgraduate Degree: a degree, usually either a Masters or Doctors in Science, Medicine, Engineering, or Architecture

The career-type variable remains unchanged.

Career Type

CT-P&S   Professionals and Scientists

CT-Admin Administrators

CT-Tec   Technicians and Semi-Professionals

Each category of the ethnolinguistic-affinity, education-level, and career-type variables is regarded as varying from 0 (absent) to 1 (present). Each category, therefore, is treated as a separate variable. Equation (2) is then rewritten.

$$S = B_0 + B_1A + B_{21}E\,1 + B_{22}E\,2 + \ldots + B_{26}E\,6 + B_{31}CT\text{-}P\&S + \ldots + B_{33}CT\text{-}TECH + B_4YS + B_{51}FR\text{-}U + \ldots + B_{54}ANG\text{-}B + U \tag{3}$$

Equation (3) will be referred to as the *general equation*.

The general equation is the one I use in the regression analysis. For statistical reasons, however, it is not possible to include both the constant term, B_0, and all the subgroups of those variables which have been broken down into dummy variables. I therefore retain the constant term and constrain one category of each of the ethnolinguistic-affinity, education-level, and career-type variables to zero. Specifically, FR-B, E2 and CT-Admin are constrained to zero by omitting these categories from the regression equation. The interpretation of results is made in terms of comparisons to the omitted category. Discussion below will make this clear.

The results of the general equation are given below. It estimates the effects of the various factors on salary level when all 296 cases are included. Later I will consider the effects of the various factors separately for each of the four ethnolinguistic categories, as well as for All Francophones and All Anglophones.

$$S = 4962.05 + 114.64(A) + \begin{vmatrix} -2293.16(E1) \\ -1422.43(E2) \\ -367.95(E4) \\ 1148.50(E5) \\ 153.86(E6) \end{vmatrix} + \begin{vmatrix} -674.01(CT\text{-}P\&S) \\ -536.08(CT\text{-}TCH) \end{vmatrix}$$

$$+ 24.40(YS) + \begin{vmatrix} -496.74(FR\text{-}U) \\ 397.12(ANG\text{-}U) \\ 337.07(ANG\text{-}B) \end{vmatrix}$$

The estimated coefficients for age, A, and years of service, YS, have the usual interpretation: other things being equal, each year of age adds \$114.64 to salary, and each year of service (seniority) adds \$24.40. As for the dummy variables, one would expect a person who has completed high school or less (E1) to receive an annual salary \$2293 lower than a man of similar other characteristics but who has a B.A. (E3, the constrained category). Similarly, a man with a post-graduate degree in, for example, arts, social sciences or law (E5) would tend to receive \$1148 more per year than the person having a B.A. (E3). Looking at the ethnolinguistic variables, the implication is that a Francophone who feels uncomfortable in English (FR-U) would receive \$497 per year less than a bilingual Francophone (FR-B); a unilingual Anglophone would receive \$397 more, and a bilingual Anglophone would receive \$337 more than a bilingual Francophone. In the different career types, we find that people both in professional and scientific and in technical careers tend to receive lower salaries than administrators—in the amounts \$674 and \$536 respectively.

Using this equation we can estimate the salary levels of men with varying combinations of characteristics. For example, we would predict that a 30-year-old civil servant, who has a bachelor's degree in arts, commerce, or social science (E3), who has been in the government employ for five years and is a bilingual Francophone would receive a salary of $8,523. The estimation is made as follows: S = 4962.05 +(114.64 x 30)+(0 x 1)+(0 x 1)+(24.40 x 5) +0 x 1 = $8523.25. By comparison we would predict that a man with the same traits except that he has only a high school education or less would earn $6,230 (i.e., $8,523.25 less $2,293.16). Similarly, a man with the above characteristics, but in a professional and scientific career would likely earn $7,849 ($8,523.25 less $674.01).

For each coefficient, its t-score, the ratio of the coefficient to its standard deviation, was computed. Using a one-tailed test at a 5% level of significance, the estimated coefficient will be significantly different from zero if the t-score exceeds 1.645. We find in the general equation that the age variable is a statistically significant factor in explaining salary (t = 5.38). We also find that education levels 1, 2 and 5 differ significantly from E3, the category constrained to zero (t = 6.26, 4.02, 3.01, respectively); that both the career variables included differ significantly from the category omitted (t for CT-P&S = 2.22, for CT-TCH = 1.75); and finally, that of the three ethnolinguistic variables included, only the unilingual Anglophone category is significantly different from the omitted category, bilingual Francophone (t = 1.66). The coefficient of multiple determination, adjusted for degrees of freedom, is .391, which is satisfactory in the analysis of cross-sectional data, and implies that we have explained about 32 per cent of the total variation in salary levels. The F-score is significant at the one per cent level, indicating that the equation taken as a whole has significant explanatory power.

To each of the dummy variable groupings (education, ethnolinguistic category, and career type) a modified version of the added variable test was applied to determine whether each has significant explanatory power.[17] Table 4.12 records the significance test information. In the general equation we note that when all variables are included each of the dummy variable categories has statistical significance.

TABLE 4.12

Significance Tests of the Dummy Variable Categories*

Regression**	Dummy Variable Category		
	Education	Career Type	Ethnolinguistic Affinity
General Equation	14.83	7.89	6.09
#1	7.05	2.91***	—
#2	4.41	1.98***	—
#3	5.38	2.20***	—
#4	8.51	0.98***	—
#5	7.80	1.05***	—
#6	1.63***	1.12***	—

* The values recorded in the table are the F-statistics.

** Regressions 1 to 6 refer to the results, by ethnolinguistic categories, presented in Table 4.13.

*** Not significant at the 5% level.

The general equation reveals some rather obvious conclusions. First, it shows that there is a positive correlation between both age and years of service, and salary attainment. Second, the general progression among the education variables from negative to positive signs indicates that level of education is directly correlated with salary.

Of more interest is the fact that the salary level of unilingual Francophones tends to be relatively low, other things being equal. However, the evidence in the general equation is more suggestive than conclusive. In order to carry out a more definitive analysis, we will have to decompose our sample into six ethnolinguistic categories: All Francophones, Unilingual Francophones, Bilingual Francophones, All Anglophones, Unilingual Anglophones, and Bilingual Anglophones. The reason for this is that in specifying the form of the general equation, as mentioned before, I have assumed that each of the explanatory variables has an independent and additive influence in determining salary. It is possible, however, that an element of interaction exists between the ethnolinguistic variable and some other explanatory variable which would obscure the independent effect

TABLE 4.13

Multiple Regression Analysis of Determinants of Salary Level of Francophones and Anglophones at the Middle Level of the Canadian Public Service (1965)

Regr. No.	Description	Constant	Age	Education Level					Career Type		Yrs. of Service	$\bar{R}^2$ [2]	F [3]	N [4]
				E1	E2	E4	E5	E6	P&S	Tech				
1	All Francophones	6115.23	78.28 (2.63)	−1595.76 (3.51)	−915.72 (2.14)	428.48 (0.94)	1274.88 (2.75)	253.45 (0.53)	−955.72 (2.41)	−481.14 (1.24)	3.61 (0.12)	.2308	5.234	128
2	Unilingual Francophones	4571.23	49.39 (2.00)	−72.73 (.131)	−74.61 (.150)	1793.83 (3.47)	1268.98 (2.54)	1213.10 (2.54)	−412.28 (.801)	811.25 (1.95)	31.14 (.98)	.5063	5.44	40
3	Bilingual Francophones	6545.71	77.00 (1.77)	−1819.47 (3.24)	−798.05 (1.43)	21.18 (.04)	1583.66 (2.61)	50.16 (.07)	−1029.86 (2.04)	−724.25 (1.46)	−3.22 (.08)	.2380	4.02	88
4	All Anglophones	4178.57	149.81 (5.13)	−2811.08 (4.99)	−1887.67 (3.38)	−969.93 (2.02)	1003.11 (1.74)	−131.54 (−0.24)	−432.06 (0.96)	−594.16 (1.27)	−34.55 (1.18)	.3455	10.80	168
5	Unilingual Anglophones	4592.18	130.48 (4.50)	−2822.22 (5.04)	−1738.18 (3.07)	−1312.58 (2.78)	1248.05 (1.58)	−604.13 (1.12)	66.59 (0.14)	−603.79 (1.31)	63.35 (2.07)	.3868	10.11	131
6	Bilingual Anglophones	1387.73	251.89 (2.47)	−3270.17 (1.76)	−2713.19 (1.60)	57.42 (.03)	1167.86 (.87)	791.97 (.45)	−1822.15 (1.45)	165.79 (.10)	−75.88 (.85)	.1691	1.814 [5]	37

1. The Education Level and Career Type variables are defined in the text. Salary, Age, and Years of Service are measured as of September 1965.
2. R^2 is the coefficient of multiple determination, adjusted for degrees of freedom.
3. F is the F-statistic.
4. The number of observations.
5. Not significant at the 5% level; all other F-scores are significant at the 1% level.

of the ethnolinguistic factor, and perhaps suggest that salary differences along these lines do or do not exist when, in fact, the opposite is true. In order to guard against this possibility I report in lines 1 to 6 of Table 4.13 the estimates of the effects of the variables for each of the ethnolinguistic categories separately.

The age factor proves very strong in all six equations. All Anglophones tend to receive almost twice as much for each passing year as do all Francophones, and broadly similar comparisons hold for the unilingual and bilingual groups. In all cases the passage of time favours the salaries of Anglophones vis-à-vis Francophones.

The seniority variable, years of service, behaves similarly. For each additional year of service an Anglophone tends to receive about $35 while a Francophone receives about $4. Perhaps more informative than the estimates of annual salary increments attributable to seniority is the fact that none of the estimated coefficients for YS in the three Francophone groups (regressions 1, 2, and 3) is significantly different from zero. The suggestion is, then, that in the case of Francophones in these organizations very little by way of salary increase can be attributed to seniority alone. For the three Anglophone groups the case is rather different. The negative sign of YS in regression 6 (bilingual Anglophones) is unexpected, but not significantly different from zero. The same variable is positive and highly significant in the case of unilingual Anglophones, and positive, though not significant for all Anglophones. Thus, while the evidence is somewhat mixed, it supports the conclusion that seniority is a relatively more important factor in determining the salary of majority than minority men.

The education variables contain uneven results. One would anticipate negative signs attaching to the E1 and E2 variables, as compared to variable E3, and positive signs for E4, E5 and E6. Furthermore, one would expect a fairly smooth progression of the magnitudes of the estimated coefficients: $B_{21} < B_{22} < B_{23} < B_{24} < B_{25} < B_{26}$. We find that the signs are generally as anticipated, but with four exceptions in thirty cases: in the E4 and E6 coefficients for all Anglophones and unilingual Anglophones. The anticipated progression is also borne out generally, but with the important exception relating to the E6 variable (a post-graduate degree in science, medicine, engineering, or architecture) whose coefficient in all cases we find to be lower than that obtained for E5 and, in five of the six equations, not to be significantly different from the constrained E3 variable. The E6 variable performed much the same way in the general equation also. Possession of this type of postgraduate degree gives one a salary not significantly larger than persons with a bachelor's degree in arts or related fields (E3). Likewise, those also having postgraduate degrees but in arts, social science, and so on (E5) generally fare better than the E6 group. Why those who could be called "Artsmen" or "generalists" do as well or better financially than these science-engineering specialists will be discussed later. But with this major exception we find the overall performance of the education variable conforms to expectations.

The estimates of the salary influence resulting from the various career types are rather mixed, but the suggestion is that the administrators tend to be more highly paid than either professionals and scientists or technicians. However, the evidence is not clear, and only three of the twelve estimated coefficients are significantly different from zero.

To sum up the results for the six equations, it appears that age and level of education consistently are significant determinants of salary attainment. One year of age, however, gives to Anglophones a salary increase generally twice as large as that obtained by Francophones. This is shown in Table 4.13, and, for education, Table 4.12 indicates that except for regression 6 (the bilingual Anglophone group), education has a significant impact on salary increases. The major exception is that persons with postgraduate degrees in science, engineering, and like fields (E6) are not at a significantly higher salary level than those with a first university degree in an arts field (E3) and are generally at lower levels than those with postgraduate degrees in arts, social sciences, and such fields (E5). Seniority makes some contribution to salary gains for Anglophones but little or none to Francophone increases. However, the contribution of one year of seniority *at the most* amounts to three-fifths of the increase from one year of age. As for the career-type variable, its effects are neither consistent nor strong and, as Table 4.12 indicates, in all six regressions this variable has insignificant explanatory power. Nonetheless I have retained the career variable in the analysis because of its theoretical importance in explaining salary, and I have retained the education variable in regression 6 in order to maintain comparability among equations.

To aid in the further investigation of the importance of the various factors in explaining salaries and, in particular, in explaining Anglophone-Francophone salary differentials, one can use the regression results to estimate the salary levels of a large number of combinations of characteristics. Altogether I estimated the salary levels for all combinations of three ages (25, 35, 45), the six education groups, the three career types, and three seniority levels (5, 10, and 15 years of service). Thus a salary level was predicted for 162 combinations of characteristics for each of the six ethnolinguistic breakdowns. However, not all of these combinations of characteristics appear reasonable. In particular, I exclude all combinations involving (1) the career type, professional and scientific, and education levels 1 and 2; (2) technicians and semi-professionals and education levels 5 and 6; and (3) young age (25 years) with long years of service (10 or 15 years). After removing these combinations we are left with 98 meaningful arrangements of variables. To locate Francophone-Anglophone differences, the salary estimates of the three Anglophone groups (All, Unilingual, or Bilingual Anglophones) were subtracted from their Francophone counterparts for each of the 98 combinations, then these differentials were examined, first to see if any were statistically significant, and second, to find any patterns in the differentials.[18]

Only 10 of the 294 (3 times 98) differentials are significantly different from zero. Every one of the 10 arises in the 45-year-old unilingual Francophone-Anglophone comparisons, and only in administrative and professional-scientific careers. Thus, although the data suggest that there are few areas revealing significant discrepancies between Francophones and Anglophones, they do pinpoint the discrepancies. Older unilingual Anglophone administrators at all seniority levels who have either a bachelors or postgraduate degree in arts or related fields (E3 or E5) have significantly higher salaries than their unilingual Francophone equivalents. Likewise, older unilingual Anglophone professional and scientific personnel with considerable seniority (10 or 15 years) and holding a bachelors or post-

FIGURE 4.5

Salary Level As Related to Age and Seniority at Two Educational Levels of Francophones and Anglophones at the Middle Level of the Canadian Public Service (1965) in Administrative or Professional-Scientific Careers

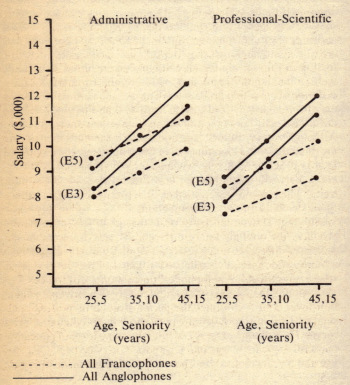

graduate degree in arts, social sciences, or other such fields (E3 or E5) are markedly better off financially than their unilingual Francophone counterparts. These, then, are the combinations of age, career type, education, and seniority where Anglophones are ahead and Francophones are lagging. Note that it is among *unilingual* Francophones that salary increases slow down. This indicates that it may not be so much an ethnic factor which accounts for the differential—Francophones who are bilingual are not significantly off the Anglophone pace—as it is lack of facility in English among these older Francophones. All in all, we find that ethnic-linguistic factors account for marked salary differentials in relatively few work areas, and in those few areas the differential may result more from an inability to function in these "English" organizations than from ethnic discrimination. Although certain factors, age and seniority in particular, bring greater gains to Anglophones than Francophones, the combined factors produce relatively few examples of gross salary differences between Anglophones and Francophones with similar traits. There is no general salary discrimination along ethno-linguistic lines in these organizations.

Although at first glance it appears that ethno-linguistic factors produce few obvious salary differentials, a close study of the pattern of differentials suggests that ethnicity and language have a more subtle impact on salary attainment. Take the two areas where significant Anglophone-Francophone differences appear: among the 45-year-olds with lengthy seniority and education level 3 or 5 in either the administrative or professional-scientific groups. Now compare to these the predicted salaries for men in the same careers and with the same level of education but with 35 years of age and ten years of service or 25 years of age and 5 years of service. The comparisons are made in Figure 4.5.

While the salary levels of young Anglophones and Francophones in administrative careers tend to be close, perhaps even favouring the Francophones, the differential turns in favour of the Anglophones as they gain in age and seniority. In fact, Anglophones with only a first university degree pull ahead of the Francophones with postgraduate degrees. Much the same pattern is present in professional and scientific careers. Here young Anglophones start a little ahead of young Francophones, and with greater age and seniority, the gap widens. Again, by age 45 Anglophones with a first university degree have surpassed Francophones with postgraduate degrees. In brief, these findings clearly show that although younger Anglophones and Francophones now start their careers with nearly equal salaries, older Francophones are significantly off the pace of Anglophone attainment. We may find no general and gross salary discrimination along entho-linguistic lines in these organizations, but we do find that older members of the Francophone minority pursuing professional scientific, and administrative careers end up in an inferior salary position.

D. Interpretation

Why is it that older minority men with seniority receive significantly lower salaries than their majority contemporaries while young minority and majority men with like characteristics receive like salaries? The obvious answer is that minority men are subject to discrimination over time and slip behind the majority men. We must, however, consider other explanations. For the process of career mobility suggested by the regression results is a mythical one, based as it is on cross-sectional data representing an amalgam of the experiences of recent recruits and old hands. The data show what would happen to young men with little seniority who miraculously during a brief period could become 45 years of age with numerous years of service. Thus the finding that the salary differential appears to grow with age could be consistent with a pattern of unequal starting salaries for men joining over the past 20 years. In this case the fact of equal pay to current juniors could eventually spell the end to salary discrimination. However, the finding could also be consistent with an equal starting salary among equals of 20 years past which has become unequal over time, in which case the differential salary pattern which we have found to exist may not disappear.

Three explanations of this inequality are often advanced. As we shall see, each explanation rests on a set of assumptions and, rather than being distinct, the explanations are intertwined. The assumptions embodied in each explanation concern the quality of the education received by minority and majority men, the rate and type of men leaving these organizations from both groups, and the workings of the promotion system.

1. *Educational Gap*: Inequality exists because the minority men who graduated a generation ago from university or college have an inferior quality of training than both their majority contemporaries in the same field and their minority fellows who graduated recently. Thus, comparisons between older minority and majority men are not made between educational equals when they appear to have the same level of training or type of degree. Now, 15 to 20 years after graduation, minority men would naturally not be at the same salary level as majority men whose training was better suited to gaining advancement. The assumptions made here are that older minority and majority men are differently trained, but that there is only random fallout from the two groups and that the promotion system moves men ahead on the basis of competence.

2. *Fallout*: This points to the fact that many of the most able minority men depart from these organizations when prospects elsewhere look brighter, leaving behind the less competent and less ambitious. Older minority personnel, those mediocre men who stuck it out, would naturally obtain lower salaries than the older majority men from whose ranks there was only a normal rate of attrition. Here, the explanation assumes similar training distributed within the two groups, but while there is random fallout from the majority group, on the minority side many capable but few incompetent men leave. The promotion system is assumed to continue working equitably.

3. *Career Discrimination*: This explanation asserts that the major cause of inequality is the working of "informal factors" which favour the majority men. The explanation assumes equivalence in the training of older minority and majority men, random fallout from both groups over time, but a promotion system which distributes benefits unequally.

Obviously none of these explanations is able by itself to

explain majority-minority differences. A synthesis is in order. I therefore briefly consider the case for each explanation, and conclude by demonstrating their interdependence.

The *Educational Gap* explanation rests largely on the fact that the Roman Catholic Church until recently provided most of the educational facilities for Francophones throughout Canada. For example, all French-language universities in Quebec were controlled by the Church. Furthermore, the Church-dominated educational system adapted slowly to the industrial economy. In 1956 a Quebec Royal Commission on Constitutional Problems, headed by Judge Joseph Tremblay, went out of its way to comment that religious groups had neither the personnel nor finances required by the expanding educational system nor the inclination to provide technical education.[19]

While it is true that the educational system for Francophones was poorly funded and underemphasized science and engineering, it was of high quality in the fields which it did stress, as I have argued in Chapter Two. The subjects emphasized were in arts, commerce, and social science—subjects regarded as ideal preparation for many positions in federal organizations. Indeed, I have already noted that a preparation in an arts or social science field tends to be more highly rewarded in the Public Service than one in science or engineering. Thus there appears to be no firm ground for the educational gap explanation, at least with reference to the arts and social science graduates.

The *Fallout* explanation derives from the rapid economic and political changes in Quebec in the early and mid-1960's. Industrial and urban growth proceeded in Quebec at much the same time and in the same pattern as in the rest of Canada.[20] From 1896 to 1913 Quebec and Canada underwent the "takeoff" into industrial development. After World War I, and particularly since 1935, a second wave of growth swept the province, reaching its peak rate in 1956. By 1921 more French in Quebec were classified as urban than as rural. As a result the economic and urban base of Quebec became quite similar to that of the rest of Canada and of other industrialized areas.

From 1944 to his death in 1959, Premier Maurice Duplessis of Quebec thwarted the working out of the immense contradiction: an industrial economy and two major urban concentrations matched with archaic, Church-controlled educational, health, and welfare systems.[21] It was the emerging urban middle class that most felt the need for change.[22] For although the major industries of Quebec were owned by Anglophones (British, American, and English Canadian), the Francophones were finding their way into middle management. More importantly, bureaucracies to service the urban population were created or enlarged. In the civil service, public utilities, marketing and distribution, construction, advertising, and mass communications, the ranks of salaried bureaucrats swelled. This emerging mass of white-collar officials in public and semi-public bodies and at the middle level of large "English" or growing "French" firms wanted to consolidate its new wealth and insure future security.[23] They sought changes in Quebec's educational, health, and welfare institutions. This meant demands on the provincial treasury, demands that Duplessis would not meet.

With the death of Duplessis in 1959 the demands of the urban middle class to redefine the function of Church and state became effective. The survival of Francophone culture and the provision of various public services, including education, were felt to be the prerogative of the provincial government and not of the Church. Jean Lesage and his Liberal Party gained the support of this middle class, came to power in 1960, and implemented changes in many spheres of Quebec society. The provincial civil service was the agent for planning and directing reforms. For the first time many talented Francophones were attracted to the provincial public service, including many able and ambitious Francophones who left the middle and upper levels of federal organizations. For example:

Many of the school's (Laval's Faculté des Sciences Sociales) graduates . . . went on to serve the federal government, not as mere trained-seal backbenchers in a well-disciplined Quebec bloc, but as top-rank civil servants in Ottawa and abroad. When the Duplessis regime crumbled and the Lesage government took power in Quebec, many of them were called back to serve the provincial government . . .[24]

There seems to have been no similar exodus from the ranks of the Anglophones during this period. Thus it appears that there is some firm support for the fallout explanation.

To recapitulate, I find some supporting evidence for the educational gap explanation of the salary differential in the case of those in science or engineering but no support in the case of those trained in arts and social sciences. There is some merit in the fallout explanation. What, then, can be said of *Career Discrimination*?

It might be possible to explain some of the difference between older Anglophones and Francophones with the same degrees in terms of an educational gap, but this hardly accounts for the fact that Anglophones with only a bachelors degree (E3) surpass Francophones with postgraduate degrees (E5). Granted that the quality of Francophone universities in a few fields was below that of Anglophone universities, it is still unrealistic to suppose that a Francophone with an M.A. or Ph.D. has received training only as good as an Anglophone with a B.A. Furthermore, 20 years after one has left university the quality of training received a generation ago would not be crucial in determining current salary. What counts more is on-the-job training and informal lore acquired in the course of one's career. Even Francophones with an inferior education could overcome this handicap if they had access to learning experiences and encouragement by superiors in the organization. That Francophones are excluded from informal training and relationships is the only way to explain how Francophones with higher degrees drop behind Anglophones with just a bachelors degree. In addition, there is no doubt that much of the fallout among Francophones occurred because of the genuine attractiveness of the positions which opened in Quebec in the early and mid-1960's. Perhaps fewer Francophones would have left Ottawa for Quebec City had the Ottawa environment provided better career opportunities. Obviously, relatively more Francophones than Anglophones not only perceived blockages to their careers but also felt that greater opportunities existed elsewhere.

There is a further finding which illuminates majority-minority relations: that Arts generalists are more financially successful than specialists with science or engineering training. These are organizations which prize the skills of policy-making or supervision. Those who possess fluency in English, interpersonal sensitivity, an outgoing and affable personality, a sociable manner on or off the job, and wide social contacts are sought after. Young men who excel in such matters are sponsored for promotion by their seniors. Obviously, Francophones who are prone to feel hesitant in the use of English and who do not share the same cultural and recreational interests as senior majority men will not often be spotted and groomed for advancement. The finding that it is among unilingual Francophones, men who perceive their linguistic skills to be faulty, that the salary disadvantage is greatest supports this observation.

It is now possible to state a final assessment of the results. First, it appears that the simple process of aging brings regular salary increments. Second, seniority has a meagre influence on salary. Third, level and type of education strongly determine the general range in which one's salary falls. But each of these statements must be qualified to take account of majority and minority status. Biological aging, the accumulation of seniority, and educational attainment bring greater gains for majority than minority men. Therefore, to answer the Weberian question raised earlier in the chapter, it appears that education (expertise) is more important for advancement than is seniority, but its effect is blunted by minority status.

In 1965 older majority men were at higher salary levels than their minority equivalents, but young majority and minority men were on a par. I have argued that although there was a fallout of able minority men in the early 1960's and an educational gap between Francophones and Anglophones in science and engineering fields, career discrimination is the primary factor accounting for the salary differentials as predicted by Hypothesis 3. Perhaps, however, the implementation of some of the recommendations of the Royal Commission on Bilingualism and Biculturalism plus the recent focus on the "French fact" in Canada will spell an end to career discrimination in the Public Service. If so the equality of salary levels which now exists for young majority and minority personnel will be maintained as they accumulate seniority.

Notes

[1]This conception borrows from Harold L. Wilensky, "Work, Careers, and Social Integration," *International Social Science Journal*, 12 (Fall, 1960), pp. 543-60, and Howard S. Becker and Anselm L. Strauss, "Careers, Personality, and Adult Socialization," *American Journal of Sociology*, 62 (November, 1956), pp. 253-63.

[2]This conception differs in emphasis but borrows some of the components of bureaucracy identified by Arthur L. Stinchcombe, "Bureaucratic and Craft Administration of Production: A Comparative Study," *Administrative Science Quarterly*, 4 (September, 1959), pp. 168-87; Stanley H. Udy, Jr., " 'Bureaucracy' and 'Rationality' in Weber's Organization Theory: An Empirical Study," *American Sociological Review*, 24 (December, 1959), pp. 791-95; Richard H. Hall, "The Concept of Bureaucracy: An Empirical Assessment," *American Journal of Sociology*, 69 (July, 1963), pp. 32-40; Richard H. Hall and Charles R. Tittle, "A Note on Bureaucracy and its 'Correlates,' " *American Journal of Sociology*, 72 (November, 1966), pp. 267-72.

[3]This theme is thoroughly treated in Harold L. Wilensky, "Orderly Careers and Social Participation: The Impact of Work History on Social Integration in the Middle Mass," *American Sociological Review*, 26 (August, 1961), pp. 521-39.

[4]Max Weber, *The Theory of Social and Economic Organization*. Translated by A. R. Henderson and Talcott Parsons (London, 1947), p. 340.

[5]Max Weber, *From Max Weber: Essays in Sociology*. Translated, Edited, and with an Introduction by H. H. Gerth and C. Wright Mills (New York, 1958), p. 203.

[6]Weber, *The Theory of Social and Economic Organization*, p. 334.

[7]See the well-known article by Melville Dalton, "Informal Factors in Career Achievement," *American Journal of Sociology*, 56 (March, 1951), pp. 407-15.

[8]*Ibid.*, p. 414.

[9]Everett C. Hughes, *French Canada in Transition* (Chicago, 1943), p. 52.

[10]*Ibid.*, p. 53.

[11]Some scholars, Wilensky for instance, would like to expand the concept of social mobility to include changes in status in areas other than the economy: acquiring a religion or an educational level different from one's parents, moving from one community to another, or a shift in ties to an ethnic community. These are all changes that can have a large effect on attitudes and behavior. Although I will restrict my discussion of mobility to changes in economic status and not refer to

these other things as cases of social mobility, I will be dealing with several of them under other headings. See Harold L. Wilensky, "Measures and Effects of Social Mobility," in Neil J. Smelser and Seymour Martin Lipset (eds.), *Social Structure and Mobility in Economic Development* (Chicago, 1966), pp. 98-140.

[12]*Ibid.*, p. 102.

[13]*Ibid.*, p. 104.

[14]The statistic is fully described in Robert H. Somers, "A New Asymmetric Measure of Association for Ordinal Variables," *American Sociological Review*, 27 (December, 1962), pp. 799-811.

[15]I am greatly indebted to Professor Byron G. Spencer for assistance in processing and interpreting the material in this section.

[16]The procedure is described in Daniel B. Suits, "Use of Dummy Variables in Regression Equations," *Journal of the American Statistical Association*, 52 (December, 1957), pp. 548-51.

[17]The test suggested by Emanuel Melichar, "Least Squares Analysis of Economic Survey Data," in American Statistical Association, *Proceedings of the Business and Economic Statistics Section*, 1965, pp. 373-85.

[18]For further details see Beattie, *et al.*, *Bureaucratic Careers*, Appendix IX.

[19]Quebec (Province), *Report of the Royal Commission of Inquiry on Constitutional Problems*, Quebec City, Government of Quebec, Volume 3, Book 1, p. 150.

[20]The details in this paragraph are from André Raynauld, *The Canadian Economic System* (Toronto, 1967), Chap. 3.

[21]Some aspects of this situation are discussed by Pierre Elliot Trudeau, "Some Obstacles to Democracy in Quebec," *Canadian Journal of Economics and Political Science*, 24 (August, 1958), pp. 297-311; Herbert F. Quinn, *The Union Nationale, A Study in Quebec Nationalism* (Toronto, 1963); and Ramsay Cook, *Canada and the French-Canadian Question* (Toronto, 1968), Chap. One.

[22]The emergence of the middle class in Quebec and their demands have been portrayed fully by Hubert Guindon. See his "The Social Evolution of Quebec Reconsidered," *The Canadian Journal of Economics and Political Science*, 26 (November, 1960), pp. 533-51 and "Social Unrest, Social Class and Quebec's Bureaucratic Revolution," *Queen's Quarterly*, 71 (Summer, 1964), pp. 150-62.

[23]Jacques Dofny and Marcel Rioux, "Social Class in French Canada," in Marcel Rioux and Yves Martin, eds., *French Canadian Society, Sociological Studies*, Volume 1 (Toronto, 1964), pp. 307-18. Originally published in French in 1962.

[24]Mason Wade, *The French Canadians, 1760-1967*, Revised Edition, in Two Volumes (Toronto, 1968), Vol. 2, p. 1113.

Chapter Five

Advancement and Assimilation

It is possible to identify a set of formal positions that appear to be the "top" of the federal administration. These are the highest-paying, most powerful posts at the apex of the various organizations which compose the Public Service. Some middle-level men aspire to such posts; most do not. Most see the top as a post in their current or related department two or three levels beyond their present level. Whatever their conception of the "top," the previous chapter showed that Francophones are likely to get there more slowly than Anglophones.

Now I want to examine in more detail the mechanisms of gaining advancement, the specific impact of linguistic and ethnic factors on promotions, and the pressures to assimilate experienced by Francophones. The connection between advancement and assimilation will be clarified. The relative influence of regional cultures and organizational cultures on assimilation will be examined. Differences between *Québecois* and Franco-Ontarians have already been made apparent; here they will be seen as fundamental. As well, the distinction between "housekeeping" organizations dealing with routine problems and creative organizations that must innovate in response to changing problems will loom large. When I have further described these two types of minority men—*Québecois* and Franco-Ontarians—and two types of majority settings—routine and creative—then the interplay between type of man and type of setting can be examined with reference to both advancement and assimilation.

A. Getting to the Top

There are three routes by which one gains entry to senior positions at the middle level or above: by an internal competition, by an open competition, or by being "parachuted" in by the government in power. Promotion from within the government department (internal competition) is the usual way of filling vacant senior positions, but, to place this procedure in perspective, I will first discuss the other two processes.

Open Competitions

Public services the world over have been established to serve as neutral instruments for the administration of government policy. One means of attaining neutrality has been to lodge the powers of appointment and promotion in the hands of an agency independent of the government in power. The aim is to eliminate meddling by politicians in the careers of public servants. Open competitions have to be seen in this light.

The open competition means that vacancies are widely advertised in the relevant geographical area (locality, region, or nationwide); all who apply and meet certain standards of age, education, and practical experience are permitted to take an examination; the person or persons who accumulates the most "merit points" is invited to fill the vacancy. The whole procedure is designed to maximize the openness of the organization by giving notice of positions to be filled to all the trained personnel in the area of competition. Although this procedure is used in recruiting recent university graduates and filling posts where a scarcity of talent exists in the Public Service, in recent years it has been employed less frequently. In the past there was a tendency in Canada and elsewhere to hold an open competition for almost every vacant position. Now the tendency is to promote or transfer within the Public Service. In fact, recent legislation (The Public Service Employment Act, 1967) enjoins the Public Service Commission, the body that oversees recruiting and staff development, to make appointments from within the federal administration except when it is not in the "best interests" of the Public Service to do so.

Parachuting

While the open competition is primarily used to recruit a substantial number of usually younger people to fill a set of similar posts, and the closed (internal) competition to move people up through the middle ranks and into the upper ranks, parachuting is often used to fill a limited number of unique posts at the top of the federal administration. These are the "political" posts that are filled by the government of the day through the mechanism of the "Order-in-Council." Included here are deputy ministers, members of boards and commissions, directors of some Crown Corporations, and Ambassadors and several other top officials in the Department of External Affairs. Many holders of these posts are lifetime civil servants. However, the party in power can and often does reach beyond the federal administration to draw in outsiders with special characteristics. Such outsiders are often brought in to meet demands from certain constituents whose support the government does not wish to lose. In recent times, the strongest demands have come from French Canada and groups that wish to see a larger representation of Francophones at the top of the federal administration. Their demands carry a large measure of validity. For, as we have seen, the career routes through the departments are filled with obstacles for Francophones. An injection of outsiders is needed at the top if a Francophone-Anglophone balance is to be maintained.

That Francophone outsiders are parachuted in at a fairly high rate is seen in several findings. First, a survey in the federal Public Service in 1965 analyzed by John W. C. Johnstone of NORC (National Opinion Research Center) at the University of Chicago found that the trend of a falling Francophone presence at successively higher salary levels is reversed at the top.[1] They compose 23 per cent of the category earning under $6,000 a year, drop steadily until they compose only 5 per cent of those in the $18,000-$19,000 range, then bounce up to 16.5 per cent of those earning $20,000 a year or more. Although technically it is possible, it did not seem that this reversal at the top came from a high promotion rate of insiders.

A second, and more pertinent finding, is drawn from results published in 1966 concerning those earning $17,000 per annum and above. A comparison can be made between the upper ranks of organizations in which Order-in-Council appointments predominate and those in which internal promotions are more likely. While in the Crown Corporations, boards, commissions, and special agencies where parachuting is both permitted and common, 16 per cent of the senior personnel were of French mother tongue, in the major departments where Order-in-Council appointments are quite restricted, 12 per cent were of French mother tongue (Table 5.1). Also noteworthy is that those of French background numbered only 6 per cent of the top civilian and military personnel in the Department of National Defence and, in the upper ranks of the physical and natural scientists at the National Research Council, there was not a single Francophone in 1966.

A third piece of evidence is drawn from a study of the Department of External Affairs.[2] Information about 570 persons, every employee who had been an officer in the Department between 1945 and 1964, was obtained. The method by which they became officers was examined.[3] While the bulk of both linguistic groups entered through open competitions (82.5 per cent of the Anglophones, 79.8 per cent of the Francophones), more Francophones than Anglophones obtained positions through Order-in-Council (12.0 per cent vs. 7.8 per cent). These Order-in-Council appointments are invariably at a senior level. Of the 49 persons who entered by Order-in-Council, 15 (or 30 per cent) were Francophones. Parachuting of Francophones is even more marked among those who obtained positions in the recent period (1958-1964): 6.9 per cent of Anglophones but 14.7 per cent of Francophones gained entry by Order-in-Council. What is more, a higher proportion of recent Francophone than Anglophone recruits enter directly at the uppermost level: in 1958-64, 9.4 per cent of Anglophones but 14.8 per cent of Francophones. Thus, the evidence appears convincing that there is an influx of Francophone parachutists to compensate for their slower progression through the middle ranks.

Closed Competitions

Closed competitions open only to public servants are the chief means of filling vacant positions in the middle and upper levels. Although they may involve objective tests given to all comers and a careful assessment of merit, many promotions are less structured. However, the rhetoric persists that the man with the

TABLE 5.1

Presence in the Upper Level (Those Earning $17,000 and Above Per Annum) of Several Sectors of the Federal Public Service of Persons of Different Mother Tongues as Reported in December 1966

| Sector | Mother Tongue | | | |
	French	English	Other	Total
21 Major Departments* (N:585)	12.3	81.2	6.5	100.0
Department of National Defence (N:187)	5.9	92.5	1.6	100.0
45 Crown Corporations Boards, Commissions, Special Agencies** (N:321)	16.2	80.7	3.1	100.0
National Research Council (N:187)	0.0	84.0	16.0	100.0
Total Public Service (N:1174)	11.5	83.0	5.5	100.0

* Dominion Bureau of Statistics is included here and counted as a separate department. The other 20 were the departments of Veterans Affairs, External Affairs, Agriculture, Insurance, Citizenship and Immigration, Trade and Commerce, Finance (including Treasury Board and the Comptroller of the Treasury), Forestry, Justice, Mines and Technical Surveys, Northern Affairs and National Resources, Fisheries, the Post Office, Defence Production, National Revenue, National Health and Welfare, the Secretary of State, Transport, Labour and Public Works.

** The following units which had personnel earning $17,000 or more a year were included: Public Archives, Unemployment Insurance Commission, Export Credits Insurance Corporation, Atomic Energy of Canada Limited, Industrial Development Bank, Bank of Canada, Crown Assets Disposal Corporation, Canadian Wheat Board, Canadian Arsenals Limited, National Capital Commission, National Battlefields Commission, Dominion Coal Board, Canadian Maritime Commission, International Joint Commission, Canada Council, Farm Credit Corporation, Defence Construction (1951) Limited, Eldorado Mining and Refining Limited, Atomic Energy Control Board, National Energy Board, Northern Canada Power Commission, National Film Board, National Gallery of Canada, Royal Canadian Mounted Police, Department of Public Printing and Stationery, Tax Appeal Board, Fisheries Research Board, Canadian Pension Com-

most "merit points" is the one chosen to do the job. Merit, in the sense of ability to do the work—the type of thing measured by objective tests—is certainly a prime consideration, but a host of new factors are brought into play. These are still defined as merit factors by the men doing the selecting, but in fact they refer to characteristics largely irrelevant to the technical content of the position to be filled. The consideration that looms largest is whether or not the candidate is liked and supported for promotion by the superiors in the work unit. In short, compatibility becomes an operative concern and sponsorship for promotion becomes a prime factor in deciding who moves up and at what rate.

Sponsorship, as Oswald Hall describes it,[4] means that established members of an organization or occupation actively intervene in the career lines of junior personnel helping them to get started and to gain promotions. Sponsorship is a process in which the senior men discover bright newcomers, show them "the ropes," give them assignments which provide crucial experience, and recommend them for positions to other senior colleagues. Naturally this process involves a good deal of learning off the job as well as on, and sociability is important. Chiefs are prone to look for bright newcomers among those who think and feel like themselves, and the proper superior-subordinate relationship is thought to flourish only when there is a good deal of social compatibility. Obviously, persons whose backgrounds, interests, and even speech patterns are different from those of their Anglophone chiefs are at a disadvantage, unless they are able to acquire the traits of the dominant group.

---

mission, Polymer Corporation Limited, National Harbours Board, Board of Broadcast Governors, Central Mortgage and Housing Corporation, Tariff Board, Canadian Overseas Telecommunication Corporation, Air Transport Board, Canadian Broadcasting Corporation, Board of Transport Commissioners, and St. Lawrence Seaway Authority. Data were not provided by the Canadian National Railways, Air Canada, and the National Advisory Council for Fitness and Amateur Sport because the officers of these bodies were not considered as public servants.

Source: Adapted from the Reply of Right Hon. L. B. Pearson (Prime Minister) to question No. 910 by Mr. Caouette, M.P., Order for Return, December 7, 1966.

The next section reveals the nature and extent of the disadvantages.

B. Language and Advancement

On the surface, Francophones who work in the Capital Region do not seem to be at a language disadvantage. Many come from Ottawa or nearby areas of Ontario where schooling and work were largely conducted in English. Some idea of the extent to which middle-level Francophones were exposed to English before joining the Public Service is suggested by the following results: while in secondary school 42 per cent received more than half their education in English, among those who attended as university undergraduates 56 per cent were in programs that were mainly English, and 61 per cent of those who attended at the postgraduate level were in "English" programs. Among middle-level Francophones who worked before entering the federal administration, 55 per cent were in an environment that was mainly English. The proportion jumps to 65 per cent when Translators are excluded.[5]

The middle-level men were asked to rate their linguistic skills in the language that was not their original one, i.e., Anglophones rated their ability in French, Francophones their ability in English. For each of several skills, they indicated their level of ability: "none," "limited—I have a great deal of difficulty," "fair—I have some difficulty," or "considerable—I have little or no difficulty." Among Francophones, 69 per cent indicated their ability to *speak* English as considerable. Seventy-nine per cent said their ability to *write* English was considerable and 85 per cent claimed considerable ability to *understand spoken* English. Nine out of ten indicated their competence in *reading* English was considerable. In each skill area—ability to speak, write, read, or understand spoken English—at least 97 per cent of the Francophones reported they had fair or considerable ability. By contrast, only 23 per cent of middle-level Anglophones reported that their skill in both reading and understanding spoken French was either fair or considerable. It is apparent, then, that most middle-level Francophones claim competence in the use of English, a competence which is almost necessary for survival in the face of the meagre competence in French possessed by the WASP majority.

The Francophones were also asked whether having to use English had ever caused them personal trouble while working in the Public Service. Fully 61 per cent of middle-level Francophones (Translators excluded) reported they had no difficulties with English.

These findings mask two things: the substantial proportion of Francophones who do experience trouble in English, and the problems posed by dependence for information on an unfamiliar, second language. First, let us take a second look at some of the findings just reported. Some 37 per cent of the Francophones were raised in the province of Quebec (outside of Hull) and most attended French schools, at least at the elementary and secondary level, while many began their worklife in French settings. Also, as many as 30 per cent of all Francophones reported that they had some difficulties in speaking English. About 20 per cent reported difficulties in writing English, 15 per cent in understanding spoken English, and 10 per cent in reading English. Even more striking is the fact that the use of English had produced or was continuing to produce difficulties in the conduct of the work of 39 per cent of middle-level Francophones (Translators excluded): 17 per cent reported that they had problems but resolved them, while 22 per cent said that they have continuing problems in being called upon to use English. Clearly, a significant proportion of Francophones are conscious of their difficulties in English.

What are the social consequences of this lack of ease in English? Brazeau has argued that dominance of one language in an organization means that the skills of those who do not know the dominant language perfectly are not developed.[6] The subordinate language group gains employment mainly in sectors where language is not important for getting work done, e.g., among operatives and technicians. Those who acquire bilingualism may fill liaison posts by which the organization is able to deal with the subordinate language group either as employees or clients. Few manage to enter administrative positions which are the best rewarded and most challenging. In short, dominance of one language means that those familiar with a secondary language are systematically excluded from the command posts in the division of labour and, as a result, are denied an adequate share of the material resources that would allow them to properly educate, or, in other ways prepare their offspring for top positions.

Thus the Francophone talent pool is not drawn on and developed. Nor are Francophones motivated to self-improvement. In the face of organizations which embody an alien language and culture and are perceived by Francophones as impenetrable and perhaps even threatening or scornful, it seems foolhardy to try to breach these barriers.[7] In short a reciprocal arrangement leading to the under-employment of Francophones emerges: their unacceptability in many senior posts because of their lack of English and specialized training means that few are highly motivated to learn English and seek the relevant training.

Besides the sociological consequences, there are psychological consequences of this situation. Nathan Keyfitz, drawing on Brazeau's findings, comments:

> Above a certain level, whether in a plant or a government office, much of the work of people goes on in relatively formal meetings, the language of which is English in the great majority of Canadian business firms. . . . There can be no question that this puts the French Canadian at a genuine disadvantage. Even the most attentive speaker of a language not his own will make a mistake now and again, and if he is sensitive this can, at least for the moment, destroy for him that indispensable image of himself as an effective person.[8]

The Francophone in an English organization develops a sense of frustration and inferiority at not being able to "put across" his ideas. What is more, many Anglophones consider his French a dialect, a style of expression far-removed from "Parisian" French and infused with many English elements. Faced with the combined problems of frustration with the use of English and being regarded as a bearer of a minor dialect, many Francophones become alienated from their work. Thus, a Francophone employee is ". . . genuinely unable to do the work as well as the English candidate wherever that work consists in large part of the manipulation of symbols in English."[9]

I have been talking in fairly general terms about the dominance of one language in a society with linguistic plurality, and of the consequences for Francophones of working in English organizations. These general processes operate, of course, no matter the degree of fluency in English that is possessed by Francophones. But there are some specific results that flow from depending on a second language for information, opinions, and enrichment. Brazeau has commented:

> There are domains of activities in which a pool of knowledge, oral and written, is not readily accessible in the minority's own tongue. As a consequence, their information is dependent on translations, never plentiful and usually bad, and their language in these areas is likely to be poor in content as well as in form. Second, as long as they remain less than fluent in the major language, less-than-perfect bilinguals may not benefit fully from the experience which they gain through their second language. . . . Among minority language groups, then, the fact that much of societal life goes on in another language may set limitations on their experience, the conceptual contents of their languages, and their manipulation of language symbols.[10]

In the Public Service, it is likely that Francophones find it difficult to gain information about and make sense of the routines, traditions, and "inside dope" of the workplace.

For Francophones the problem of adjusting to this English milieu is quite formidable. Even those who stay on, make an effort to use English competently, and work as hard as possible, are often frustrated at promotion time, as Keyfitz points out:

> There is a tendency for the English to judge the French not by the breadth of their vision, nor by their ability to communicate, but by their mastery of the intricacies of English usage and vocabulary and even by their pronunciation of English. Since the French in judging one another attach very little weight to speaking English at all and none whatsoever to whether it is spoken with a good accent, they will, as far as this element is concerned, arrange one another in a different order of merit from that in which the English arrange them. This raises the possibility that in a system of search for

ability in which English speakers make the choices they not only choose too few French but they also do not choose the right ones.[11]

If a promotion involves, as E. C. Hughes suggests,[12] superiors giving a ''vote of confidence'' to one of their juniors, then senior Anglophones may be prone to back a Francophone, not so much for his technical competence, as for his fluency and ease in sociability in the English language.

All Francophones are subject to one or more of these penalties in competing for promotions in organizations where Anglophones dominate the top positions. Sponsorship is less readily available and the process of evaluation is stacked against them. The penalties, however, are not evenly distributed among all Francophones. Some have more, or more serious, linguistic problems than others. Here the distinction between *Québecois* and Franco-Ontarians becomes crucial.

C. Types of Minority Men

The two types of minority men—*Québecois*, Franco-Ontarians—are rather differently equipped to handle the language regime of these English organizations. *Québecois* grew up in areas where the Francophone minority was dominant. Although on a Canada-wide scale Francophones are a minority, in the Province of Quebec they are a numerical majority and control many major institutions in the province: provincial government and its public service, most educational institutions, most hospitals, most newspapers, several television outlets, and many economic enterprises. Anglophones do control most of the large manufacturing and financial institutions and have access to education, health services, mass media, and retail outlets operated in English, but the French language is the dominant one in the province. Francophones in Quebec have ready access to French education, mass media, and political organs. Those who come to the federal administration in the National Capital have a solid formal education in French and extensive involvement in the culture of Quebec. Yet despite this immersion in French-language institutions and the considerable linguistic problems involved in working in these English organizations, they tend to enter workplaces where the need to know English and the pressure to assimilate are greatest. *Québecois* seem prepared to move out of their ethnic world in pursuit of career ambitions, as we shall see.

Franco-Ontarians, compared to the *Québecois*, as Paul-André Comeau points out,[13] are a double minority: as Francophones they are a minority in the Canadian nation, but also, in the regions of Ontario where they are concentrated, they play a meagre part in economic and political life. The French language is hardly acknowledged at all in the provincial government and until recently, there was no public education in French, although the Roman Catholic Church, with its separate school system, did maintain some French schools. To add to their troubles, Franco-Ontarians are clustered in parts of the province that are either rural or economically underdeveloped, or offer employment chiefly for operatives in extractive industries (mining, lumbering). Franco-Ontarians, therefore, grow up in areas that are impoverished both in general economic development and in the development of French-language institutions (schools, newspapers, companies, stores, professional services). As a consequence, the Franco-Ontarians fare badly in obtaining an education, particularly when only English schools are readily available (see Chapter 2), yet they become adept at living in an English environment. Those who obtain federal posts at the middle-level in the Capital Region enter with considerable competence in the use of English, yet they gravitate to settings where the pressures to use English and to assimilate are not as great. Perhaps as an outcome of being a "double minority," those Franco-Ontarians concentrated in settings which allow for the expression of a French identity—the vast majority of Franco-Ontarians—tend to retain strong ties in the ethnic community, as we shall see.

The difference in linguistic skills between the *Québecois* and Franco-Ontarians at the middle level can be highlighted by several findings. These indicate that although the federal administration presents some linguistic problems to the Franco-Ontarians, to the *Québecois*, entering government service in the Capital must be a traumatic step. For instance, while 78 per cent of those from the Ottawa-Hull area claim considerable ability in speaking English, only 51 per cent of the Quebecers (excluding Hull) do so (Figure 5.1). Almost half of the *Québecois*, then, feel they have some or a lot of difficulties in speaking English. In a work environment where verbal skills are essential, this is an important indicator of disadvantage. In addition, in response to a direct question about language problems at work, 56 per cent of the *Québecois* report problems with English that made or continues to make their work difficult to perform. The comparable figure for Franco-Ontarians is 30 per cent. In short, it is the Francophones from Quebec, the heartland of French Canada, who experience the most trouble in adjusting to the linguistic dominance of English in the federal Public Service.

One is led immediately to ask why it is that Francophones, particularly the *Québecois*, are willing to suffer the linguistic penalties associated with employment in English organizations. Earlier, in the chapter on joining the federal administration (Chapter 3), the factors behind their decision were briefly discussed. Here, I want to place these findings in perspective.

The allocation of trained personnel to occupations and organizations is an outcome of two processes: personal selection and organizational selection.[14] Personal selection refers to preferences of individuals for certain types of employment. Such preferences are largely the result of early socialization in the family, ethnic-religious community, and student groups. Organizational selection refers to the recruitment preferences of organizations. Organizational recruiters in their search for new personnel look for persons not only of a certain age, training, and experience but also of a preferred sex, ethnic-religious membership, class background, and perhaps, even with attendance at a certain training institution. Thus, the presence of a person in an occupation or workplace is an outcome of both personal and organizational selection. Obviously, the two processes do not operate in isolation. Preferences acquired by a person in early life reflect the realities of the economy. One does not usually strive for a position where the possibilities of failure or being rejected are high. Conversely, the recruitment preferences of an organization or occupation become known and those who fit the requirements feel confident in applying. When recruiters try to hire a type of person different from the usual sort

FIGURE 5.1

Percentage of Francophones at the Middle Level of the Canadian Public Service (1965) Who Claim Considerable Skill in English by Geographical Origin

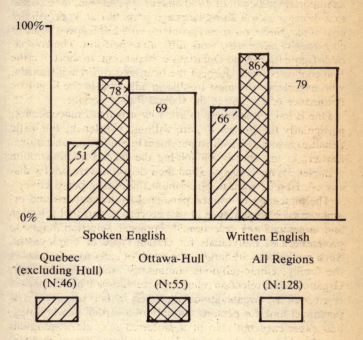

they take on, the narrowness of their recruitment base is made obvious to them.

The processes of personal and organizational selection have been clearly demonstrated in law.[15] Those who grow up in a Jewish or Catholic family and aspire to be a lawyer are likely to acquire a preference for a certain type of law school and legal career. Catholics gravitate to Catholic schools while Jews, until recently told about quotas and rebuffs at famous schools, chose second-class places. The ethnic culture of both groups tends to emphasize individual entrepreneurship. By contrast, sons of wealthy Protestant families aspire to enter the best schools and pursue a career in a large firm. Recruiters from large firms seek out graduates from the top schools[16] while the concentration of Catholics and Jews in solo practice means that recent graduates with the same background are likely to find this the easiest route to follow.[17] The interplay between the two processes is also obvious. The value placed on individual entrepreneurship is in part a response to the desire to avoid discrimination in large firms. The fact that lawyers of minority background gravitate to second-class law schools also means that they do not come to the notice of the large firms. Other reciprocal processes could be mentioned. The main point, however, is that it is important to consider both personal preferences and organizational recruitment in accounting for the relative presence or absence of certain types of persons in occupations or careers.

Chapter 3 revealed that Franco-Ontarians entered government employment to obtain security while *Québecois* were more likely to see the federal administration as a place where challenging work was available. These ambitions become understandable in the light of the backgrounds of the personnel in the two groups. Franco-Ontarians, raised in areas that were economically impoverished and blocked from attaining advanced schooling, would be prone to seek out secure employment. *Québecois*, with a higher level of education and a greater range of employment possibilities, would be concerned about putting their skills to good use. Clearly, then, the personal preferences of those in the two regional groups are different. But what are the recruitment preferences of the organizations which they enter? This is the explanatory task of the next section and will complete the description of the processes of personal and organizational selection.

D. Types of Majority Settings

The five organizations included in this study were chosen to represent the range and diversity of the federal administration. Although each organization is dominated by an English Protestant group, they differ markedly in operating style. Two categories become clear: departments where routine, repetitive activities predominate in a subdued atmosphere contrasted with departments where creative tasks are performed in a workplace that participants view as exciting. In delineating this distinction further, I was aided by some ideas presented by Charles Perrow.[18] Perrow ranges organizations along two dimensions: the number of exceptional or "rare" cases and problems that must be handled, and the degree to which solutions to exceptions are arrived at by logical analysis or systematic research. Routine predominates in organizations or units where there are few exceptional cases or problems and where there are fixed procedures or programmes to guide the search for a solution to those exceptions that do occur. Creativity predominates in organizations where there are many unique and different problems tackled and where the problems are so general and poorly conceptualized as to require intuition and guesswork for their solution.

Supplied with Perrow's guidelines and my own "feel" for the type of work and emotional mood of the organizations, I arrived at a tentative classification. Most of the sectors in the Departments of Finance and Agriculture were clearly near the creative pole. The former department is small and contains highly-educated men (mainly economists) who carry out analyses of economic problems and develop policies. The latter is dominated by a large sector of agricultural scientists; those not in the science sector are predominantly policy-makers or professionals. The remaining three departments were placed in the routine category. National Revenue (Taxation Division) mainly processes tax returns and serves the public; Public Works personnel administer regional offices that, in turn, supervise construction projects; and the Secretary of State contains two large stodgy units: the Patent Office, where patent applications were examined and classified, and the Translation Bureau, whose employees were responsible for rendering English tests into French, or vice-versa (a job which some argue will soon be done by machine).

Other findings supported the classification. Finance and Agriculture were relatively "new" departments, and embodied modern technologies. Finance was greatly altered and expanded during and after the Great Depression and has kept in close touch with developments in economic analysis in the academic world. Agriculture, also, is in touch with and operates very much on the model of academic research agencies. It has a long history of serving the agricultural industry but it is only since World War II that it has become the major centre for certain types of biological research and agricultural control. The other three departments have been in existence for over 100 years with few changes in basic function; only the scope and techniques of their work have changed, and these but gradually in comparison to the other two departments. When I classified the personnel in the five departments according to whether their work was primarily creative or routine, the findings supported the distinction (Table 5.2).

It will be recalled that middle-level Francophones tend to be concentrated in routine settings (Public Works, National Revenue [Taxation], Secretary of State) and are under-represented in creative settings (Finance, Agriculture). Francophones in each department also tended to be lower participants in terms of salary and occupational attainment. Findings for the whole federal administration confirm this situation. First, if we take as a standard the overall contribution of the French group to the federal departments—22 per cent of all personnel—we find that they are bunched near the bottom of the occupational hierarchy.[19] In most departments, more than 22 per cent of those in lower positions (persons earning under $10,000 a year in 1965) were of French background, but in only two departments, the Post Office and Secretary of State, were more than 22 per cent of the top personnel (persons earning $10,000 a year or more) French. Both these departments provide routine services and are of limited national influence. Francophones are virtually absent from the higher levels of the important and dynamic departments: Finance, Trade and Commerce, Agriculture, and Transport. Second, although Francophones are generally below the 22 per cent standard in managerial and professional occupations, they are over-represented in areas where there are strict and known rules of adequate performance. Such is the occupation of Translator. Another is the lawyer. Interestingly, a third of government lawyers are Francophones.[20] All this raises the question of why Francophones are not recruited for creative work but instead are concentrated in routine activities.

Basically the answer concerns questions of power and au-

TABLE 5.2

Per Cent of Personnel in Routine or Creative Work Areas Among Francophones and Anglophones at the Middle Level of the Canadian Public Service (1965) by Department

Department and Linguistic Group	Type of Work Activity		
	Routine (Technical, Engineering and Lower-Administrative Personnel.)	Creative (Scientific or Policy-Making Personnel.)	Total
Finance			
Francophones (N:6)	17	83	100
Anglophones (N:28)	18	82	100
Agriculture			
Francophones (N:28)	43	57	100
Anglophones (N:37)	30	70	100
Public Works			
Francophones (N:28)	75	25	100
Anglophones (N:32)	88	13	101
National Revenue			
Francophones (N:33)	97	3	100
Anglophones (N:33)	94	6	100
Sec. of State			
Francophones (N:33)	94	6	100
Anglophones (N:38)	87	13	100

tonomy. The Anglophones hold power; the Francophones are subject to their decisions. Following Weber and Kaplan, a group A has power over group F, if members of A, when they wish, can affect the probability that members of F will behave in a certain way in certain circumstances.[21] Members of A may have great power over persons in F and produce highly probable acts—up to the 1.0 level where Fs always do what As wish—or their power may be slight—down to the .01 or .001 level where Fs react somewhat to As' wishes but they are also affected by other "powers." In the present case, Anglophones desire to circumscribe the choices and possibilities of Francophones in the federal administration. Such power, however, is reduced in creative work. Obviously, when the problems dealt with are unique and require inventiveness and intuition, employees have a maximum of personal autonomy. To use intuition and guess-work is to make full use of one's personality and cultural background. Supervisors have to be able to trust their subordinates to work independently and fruitfully. Such a situation is difficult to maintain when Anglophone superiors confront Francophones with backgrounds and interests different from their own.

Creative work also involves extensive communication among employees. Ideas are traded around and a great deal of discussion goes on both on and off work. Unless a person is adept at informal communication and is thoroughly wrapped up in his work, this sort of give-and-take will not take place. Francophones, with their linguistic handicaps, are not going to be recruited for such work by the Anglophone bosses. The upshot is that Anglophones recruit Francophones for routine settings where their activities are circumscribed and their performance easily assessed while creative work remains an Anglophone preserve. Those Francophones who do gain entry are subject to considerable pressure to become fluent in English and to be interested in discussing their work both during and after office hours. This aspect of creative work will become clearer when I discuss assimilation in the next section.

Studying these organizations in terms of power and autonomy brings us, according to Michel Crozier, to the "new central problem of the theory of organization."[22] Early theorists viewed organizations as rational machines; the employees were regarded as each providing a pair of willing hands that helped the organization accomplish its prime goal. Later theorists who emphasized human relations—Mayo, Roethlisberger, Whyte—saw employees as emotional beings. "A human being, however, does not have only a hand and heart. He also has a head, which means that he is free to decide and play his own game."[23] Thus, argues Crozier, students of organizations who examine relations between groups (administrative units, skill or ethnic groups) must see each one trying to impose order and predictability on the ones with which it deals; each one, on the other hand, tries to curtail the influence of others on itself so that it maintains freedom, and other groups remain uncertain as to how it will act. The subgroups of an organization are compelled by the organizational design to blend their activities together in order to accomplish the organizational goals, but each subgroup attempts to exercise power over others by imposing routines on them and keeping them uncertain as to when and how it will behave. Both the unwillingness of Anglophones to recruit Francophones for units doing creative work and the concentration of Francophones in settings and occupations where routine activities predominate can be understood using Crozier's perspective.

E. The Interplay Between Minority Type and Majority Setting

I have discussed in broad terms the processes of personal and organizational selection. Franco-Ontarians, skilled in English but with meagre formal training, seek out security of employment. *Québecois*, lacking in English skills but with considerable education, want a challenging assignment. Routine organizations welcome Francophones, while creative organizations discourage them unless their English is good. Now we can see how both types of minority men fare in both types of majority settings. I will chiefly be interested in the degree to which minority men maintain or shed ties to their ethnic-linguistic community.

In a study of professors, lawyers, and engineers, Wilensky and Ladinsky postulate that the interplay between minority men and majority setting is quite straightforward:

> . . . we would expect successful minority men who find themselves in majority contexts—occupations and work-places dominated by established Protestant elites—to epitomize the process of structural assimilation; in their ties to kin, friend and formal association, they should be escaping from the religious community of origin and moving into the occupational or corporate community of destination. [24]

This supposition is clearly supported by the authors' data: "Apparently these men head toward a majority context, drop religious identification and its main prop, minority friends and relatives, and then arrive at their present jobs in law firm, corporation, and university." [25] However, the Canadian scene reveals a variation on this theme.

In general, it is in the more senior posts, and especially posts in creativity-oriented departments, that the pressure is greatest on Francophones to use English. Figure 5.2 shows that acquisition of status as indicated by a move from one salary level to a higher one is tantamount to a decrease in the opportunity to use French, whatever the area of work. Also, the few Francophone policy-makers and scientists, concentrated chiefly in the departments of Finance and Agriculture report they are able to use French very little on the job, compared with the employees in Public Works and National Revenue (mainly technicians, semi-professionals, engineers and lower-administrators). Twenty-eight per cent of Francophone scientists and policy-makers, but 56 per cent of the technical, semi-professional, engineering, and lower-administrative employees say they make substantial use of French at work.

Now to the main anomaly: the Franco-Ontarians, with their incomplete education but competence in English, are concentrated in those routine departments and careers where there is large scope for the use of French, while the *Québecois*, weak in English but with good educational credentials, are concentrated in the creative work settings where the opportunity to use French is lessened. Sixty-four per cent of the Francophone middle-level

FIGURE 5.2

Percentage of Francophones at the Middle Level of the Canadian Public Service (1965) Who Make Substantial Use of French at Work by Career Type and Salary Level

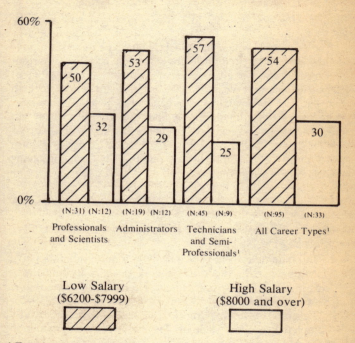

Low Salary
($6200-$7999)

High Salary
($8000 and over)

[1] Translators are excluded.

in Public Works and 73 per cent in National Revenue are from Hull, Ottawa or elsewhere in Ontario. By contrast, half of the Francophone personnel in Agriculture comes from Quebec, excluding Hull. Similarly, 46 per cent of Francophones in the relatively routine areas of technical, semi-professional, engineering, and lower-administrative work are from the Ottawa-Hull region, but 32 per cent of the scientific and policy men. In short, Franco-Ontarians are the predominant type of Francophone in routine work settings where French can be used while *Québecois* are over-represented among Francophone employees in settings where creative work is the order of the day and the use of French is limited. Apparently, Franco-Ontarians, who would face fewer problems in creative settings where English is especially emphasized, do not enter these settings while *Québecois*, who have far greater problems with English, do seek entry.

The ease with which the Franco-Ontarians move into government circles is exemplified by Case 1, a composite portrait constructed from many interviews with these sorts of men. Raised in Ontario, especially in the area immediately adjacent to Ottawa, with French background and a low level of schooling, these men have limited employment opportunities. They are pleased at getting a secure government job with the prospects of advancement. Case 2, which depicts a standard career pattern for a *Québecois*, amply brings out the linguistic problems *Québecois* men confront.

Case 1.   *Francophone Technical Officer*

In his middle forties, B. serves in a quasi-administrative position where he supervises a work group of technical officers in a large stable department. He has been in the Public Service for about 25 years and earns around $8,000 (1965).

B. grew up in the Ottawa-Hull region and successfully completed secondary school. The summer of his graduation he went to work for his uncle in a small grocery store, but the business was too small and there was little to do. Looking for a temporary job he automatically gravitated toward the government. ". . . le fédéral était le 'gros' employeur dans le temps:" B. began at the Clerk I level and has remained with the service ever since.

From this humble beginning the career history of B. has been one of a steady but unspectacular upward climb. Early in his career he tried a competition, and successfully jumped two grades. His new duties involved processing technical documents, and he stuck to this work area. A few years later there was a promotion to chief clerk in his section, and soon thereafter a reclassification gave him a new title of Technical Officer. Since 1952 he has had five promotions. He now states proudly that he earns the top salary of those in his division who are non-professionals.

Asked where he will go from here, B. remarks, without bitterness, that he has reached his peak. He lacks educational qualifications for a professional status and isn't interested in the struggle to attain them. However, on departmental urging he recently took a course in administration. He feels this has helped broaden his outlook.

When asked what he thinks the recent emphasis on bilingualism in the Public Service will mean, B. is vague. It won't affect him personally. But perhaps it will make things better for others. He went on to state:

Le service civil sera plus fort. Avec le travail dans les deux langues, les deux auront à gagner. Les Anglais et les Français auront à gagner, autant à travailler en français qu'en anglais. Au début je n'aimais pas les Anglais à première vue. Mais une fois qu'on les connaît, on change d'idée.

With regard to his career in the Public Service, the dominant impression B. gives is one of contentment. He is satisfied with the promotion system, and has been well served by it. According to B. there is no discrimination as long as Francophones had "la maîtrise et la connaissance de la langue anglaise." He is happy in his work. Above all, he is happy that his progress in the Public Service has allowed him to provide a good home for his family in Hull. He wouldn't think of leaving the Ottawa-Hull area, where he has lived all his life.

Case 2. *Francophone Administrator-Professional*.

D. is a man in his late thirties with roughly fourteen years of experience in the federal Public Service. He is an administrator in a large service department earning a little over $9,000 a year (1965).

D. grew up in Quebec City. Because of financial difficulties he had to discontinue his university education. He originally planned to go into law, but settled for a lesser profession, accountancy. After working and attending night school for six years he finally received his diploma. D's original design was to secure a position using his speciality in a large English-owned firm but one that afforded Francophones a chance to work in French. But nothing materialized. For a short time things were quite difficult for him and his family. Then he spotted a Public Service competition for specialists in his field. He took the competition, did well, and entered the department in which he is presently employed. His first job was in a regional office in a small Quebec city. Asked why he joined the Public Service he states: ''J'étais à pied, et le salaire était plus intéressant que celui de l'entreprise privée.''

D. remained in his first Public Service job for two years; then, after entering a competition, he received a promotion and a transfer to Montréal. At this stage D. felt he was making progress in his career, and was also developing skill in English.

The next years were happy ones for D. Warming quickly to city existence, he joined clubs and associations, and he and his wife were active socially. He settled down and was content to stay. However, after six years, an administrative position with some policy-making duties became vacant in Ottawa, and Head Office approached him. D. was a little reluctant to leave his Montréal situation, but his superiors painted a very rosy picture of his future.

D. made the move to Ottawa five years ago, but somewhere along the line his career went sour. In spite of trying numerous competitions, the promotions he expected never came. D. is particularly bitter about the top post in a regional office he failed to get. The post, according to D., clearly called for a bilingual person and someone who had extensive knowledge of the region. D. met both these requirements, nevertheless an inexperienced unilingual ''anglais'' got the job. D. cited other cases similar to this one. In his view ''le fait d'être Canadien français semble être un obstacle.'' He feels it is discrimination, but also admits that his English and lack of rapport with senior personnel may have held him back.

In D.'s work relations there are some satisfactions. He does work almost completely in English but has been able to acquire close friends at the office. He has also purchased a home in Ottawa and has become friendly with some of his English neighbours. With his 14 years of pension payments, he expects he will stay with the government despite his current problems.

What the case studies do not show is that although Franco-Ontarians adjust easily to majority settings, the strength of their ethnic ties varies between routine and creative settings. Routine work fosters ethnic ties, while creative work weakens them. However, since Franco-Ontarians are both absolutely and relatively few in number in creative settings, the maintenance of ethnic ties for the group as a whole is great. *Québecois*, concentrated as they are in creative settings, experience a greater overall erosion of ethnic ties. Let me spell this out in more detail.

An indication of the strength of one's ties to an ethnic community is the ethnic allegiance of one's best friends. I asked the middle-level Francophones to report the ethnicity of their three best friends. Clear differences do not appear in inter-organizational comparisons (Table 5.3), but there is a tendency for relatively more persons in the rather routine settings of Public Works, National Revenue, and Secretary of State to report that all three of their three best friends are Francophones, than in either Agriculture or Finance.[26] The tendency is more striking when the data are regrouped in slightly different ways. First, Table 5.4 shows the results for career specialties. Clearly the men in routine fields maintain much closer ties to their ethnic brethren. Those in creative fields are more likely to draw their friends from outside the French-Canadian sector. And second, this applies as much to the non-Quebecers as to the Francophones from Quebec who are concentrated in these fields:

TABLE 5.3

Per Cent Indicating that Their Three Best Friends Are All Francophones Among Francophones at the Middle Level of the Canadian Public Service (1965) by Department

Department	Per Cent Indicating Three Best Friends Are All Francophones
Finance (N:6)	17
Agriculture (N:28)	43
Public Works (N:28)	46
National Revenue (N:33)	55
Secretary of State (N:38)	63
Total Francophones (N:128)	50

TABLE 5.4

Per Cent Indicating that Their Three Best Friends Are All Francophones Among Francophones at the Middle Level of the Canadian Public Service (1965) by Career Type

Career Type	Per Cent Indicating Three Best Friends Are All Francophones
Scientists (N:14)	21
Policy-Makers (N:17)	29
Technicians and Engineers (N:30)	50
Semi-Professionals (N:51)	61
Lower-Administrators (N:16)	63
Total Francophones (N:128)	50

38-39 per cent of the Francophones in the dynamic atmosphere of Finance and Agriculture whether from Quebec or outside it report that all their friends are French, but 50 per cent of both geographic groups in the stodgy environments of Public Works and National Revenue do so. Creative settings weaken the ethnic ties of those Francophones (mainly *Québecois*) who choose to enter, while routine settings allow Francophones (mainly Franco-Ontarians) to maintain their ethnic allegiances. Let me rephrase this a little differently: in routine settings, where most Franco-Ontarians and a few *Québecois* are found, the assimilation pressures are weakest, while in creative settings, where the Francophones (few as they are) are chiefly from Quebec, the pressure to assimilate is much stronger.

So far I have suggested that work overcomes minority ethnic-religious ties not in all majority contexts, but chiefly in creative ones. Let me temper somewhat this emphasis on organizational pressures to assimilate. There is a suggestion that assimilation-prone men gravitate toward creative work. Organizational pressures may simply serve to reinforce a tendency that began early in a person's life. Despite the extra linguistic handicaps associated with creative work, those Francophones who enter this area seem already predisposed to move out of their ethnic world. The main evidence concerns choice of a marriage partner and is presented in Table 5.5. Married men doing creative work—scientists and policy-makers—are less likely to have a French wife than are persons in routine fields (technicians and engineers, semi-professionals, and lower administrators). Either before or soon after arriving in majority settings where creative work is done, these Francophones had been drawn out of their ethnic subsociety in their choice of a wife and were likely assimilation-prone. Thus, both self-selection and organizational processes appear to lie behind the weakening of ethnic ties among Francophones in creative settings.

It is apparent that there are two parallel streams of incorporation of the French-Canadian minority into English-dominated work settings. One follows the process identified by Wilensky and Ladinsky for minority men who work alongside WASPish professors, lawyers, and engineers (called "deviant ethnics" by the authors). Those in Dynamic work settings (mainly educated

TABLE 5.5

Per Cent With a Wife of French Origin Among Married Francophones at the Middle Level of the Canadian Public Service (1965) by Career Type

Career Type	Per Cent With Wife of French Origin
Scientists (N:13)	69
Policy-makers (N:14)	57
Technicians and Engineers (N:26)	77
Semi-Professionals (N:41)	85
Lower-Administrative (N:15)	80

Québecois) are prone to set aside ethnic ties and mix with English colleagues both on and off the job, despite the language troubles this occasions. Those concentrated in routine sectors that are also English-dominated, however, find that they can "fit" linguistically into the work activity, especially since most are Franco-Ontarians who acquired English in early life; yet they are not motivated to abandon their ethnic roots.

F. Implications

My findings suggest that in certain majority settings the assimilation of minority men is an almost irresistable process, while in other settings, ethnic ties can remain strong. Assimilation tendencies are strong among minority lawyers in legal firms, professors in universities, and engineers in large corporations as Wilensky and Ladinsky have shown. My data indicate that the same process unfolds for Francophones in English policy-making and biological-research units. All these settings and occupations have four features in common. The men in them have invested a long period of time in getting advanced training and seem to be highly motivated to get into workplaces where they can use their skills to best advantage. They are strongly career-minded. Second, they are in fields where it is difficult to separate work and non-work; the intense involvement with work does not end at five o'clock. Discussion with one's colleagues tends to flow into off-work friendships. Third is the importance of verbal fluency in presenting ideas to others, personal style, and being hooked into the organizational "grapevine"; in short, human relations and interpersonal skills are crucial. Finally, and related to the previous point, promotion in these fields not only involves demonstrated competence but is facilitated by being spotted and sponsored by one's superiors. Those in the command posts in the work setting ultimately encourage or deny promotion on the basis of whether they regard the man as having the personal qualities that they wish to see in colleagues.[27] This means that the development of rapport with persons higher on the hierarchy is fundamental for advancement. Obviously each of these features fosters assimilation.

In middle-level and some senior, but not top, posts in government and industry where minority men are in an "alien" environment, the maintenance of an ethnic identity and links with an ethnic community remain possible. These are chiefly professional, semi-professional, technical, and supervisory posts: draftsmen, designers, computer programmers, lab-technicians, lower-administrative personnel (the ethnic man-in-the-middle has often been commented on), and certain types of professionals (engineers, accountants, lawyers) who stick to their technical tasks and avoid becoming the "organization man." Again, there are several obvious reasons explaining the persistence of ethnic identity among such men as compared to those in high-flying creative fields. First, there is less personal investment in getting an education. These men are not as highly motivated to "make it" as are the men seeking a financial return on their educational capital. Second, these technical and supervisory activities do not carry over into one's extra-work life. It is possible to segregate work activities from activities with kin and neighbourhood friends and thus move outside one's occupational community in off-work hours. Third, the central feature of this work is the dependable, consistent performance of a relatively routine technical function. A "pleasing personality" is not a primary emphasis. And, fourth, promotions in these sections are awarded to the few who demonstrate technical proficiency in a relatively open contest. It is quiet, conscientious and skilled performance that brings one to the attention of one's superiors. In sum: these occupations and careers allow for the persistence of ethnic identity; they do not generate strong pressure to be shaped in the majority mould, thus confirming Hypothesis 4.

When such features are present in a career or work organization the preservation of links to an ethnic community remains possible for minority men in majority contexts. But there are two forces outside the economic sphere which provide additional props for ethnic identity. If a person is able to live in an ethnic neighbourhood or, at least, be geographically close to a large number of his co-ethnics, then it is easier to maintain ethnic links outside working hours. This is clearly shown in the case of the Franco-Ontarians. They could live quite comfortably in Hull, or be close enough to relatives to visit regularly. Quebecers felt uncomfortable in Hull, dominated as it was by the English language, and were usually far from family and friends in Montreal, Quebec City, or the population belt along the St. Lawrence River. Many regarded living in Ottawa as not much different from living in Hull since the latter was so infused with English media. This, of course, hastened their acclimatization to English culture. But the general point is that the availability of either a large number of one's fellow ethnics living together in a separate part of town, or of one's family of origin, or both, can encourage the continued identification with one's ethnic roots.

The second support for minority identity is the degree of legitimacy and respect accorded one's ethnic group by members of the dominant ethnic group. If the revelation of one's ethnic origins occasions negative reactions, then one's ethnic roots will be played down. In Canada where the legitimacy of being French Canadian is not questioned and there is even worried concern among senior Anglophones about the fate of their Francophone brethren, it is quite proper to demonstrate one's Gallic propensities. And the same applies to other ethnic groups in Canada and the United States: when the members of the majority group with whom a person works place no stigma on his ethnic roots, and, in fact, may regard his "people" as deserving of good treatment, then it is more likely that a person will feel at ease in keeping up his ethnic connections.

What I am urging, at base, is more caution to those who argue that the WASPy settings that dominate the economy and federal Public Service will inevitably engulf the minority men who dare to enter. Among minority men who are in work sectors outside the key policy-making, administrative, or fact-gathering units in a majority setting, the continuance of an ethnic identity will not be strongly challenged. When, in addition, the minority person is able to maintain ties in a nearby and relatively thriving ethnic community, and is able to be unashamed of his roots, then the preservation of his connections with his ethnic past will be further enhanced. Thus a conclusion like the following is overly pessimistic:

> If our deviant ethnics are typical, this [mixing of ethnic groups] will not be the social and cultural blending of the "melting pot," nor the autonomy of "cultural pluralism," but old-fashioned Anglo-Conformity, which remains the most common form of assimilation, in practice if not in ideology. For the new men in higher circles, occupation will not merely be a way of life; it will be the death of the religious community.[28]

Yet, even after making this harsh conclusion, the same authors suggest briefly that there are some majority settings where minority men can preserve their identity. Those in occupations with weak professionalism which emphasize dedicated service to the employer, e.g., Catholic engineers in Protestant companies, do not feel the clash between ethnic-religious and work obligations. I heartily agree that it is just such settings that permit ethnic-religious culture to survive. Since the bulk of the persons in most organizations are in routine rather than creative work, the future of ethnic diversity seems assured. Structural pluralism will continue as an integral part of North American life, drawing strength even from minority men whose work draws them into majority settings if of the routine type.

Notes

[1]John W. C. Johnstone, *et. al.*, *A Survey of the Canadian Public Service*, a research report prepared for the Royal Commission on Bilingualism and Biculturalism, Ottawa, 1966.

[2]Gilles Lalande, *The Department of External Affairs and Biculturalism*, a study prepared for the Royal Commission on Bilingualism and Biculturalism, Ottawa, 1969.

[3]*Ibid.*, Chap. Two.

[4]Oswald Hall, ''The Informal Organization of the Medical Profession,'' *Canadian Journal of Economics and Political Science*, 12 (February, 1946), pp. 30-44.

[5]Translators compose 18 per cent of the Francophone sample at the middle level. The education, prior work history, and present working language of this group are almost exclusively French. They are also largely isolated in one special workplace—the Translation Bureau —where French predominates. I have therefore left them out of some of the calculations in order to give a more accurate picture of Francophones in ''English'' organizations.

[6]E. Jacquès Brazeau, ''Language Differences and Occupational Experience,'' *The Canadian Journal of Economics and Political Science,* 24 (November, 1958), pp. 532-40. It is reprinted in Marcel Rioux and Yves Martin (eds.), *French-Canadian Society*, Volume I (Toronto: 1964), pp. 296-307. The page references in the following footnotes are to the latter source.

[7]This is discussed by Guy Rocher, ''Research on Occupations and Social Stratification,'' in Rioux and Martin (eds.), *French-Canadian Society*, pp. 328-41.

[8]Nathan Keyfitz, ''Canadians and Canadiens,'' *Queen's Quarterly*, 70 (Winter, 1963), pp. 170-71.

[9]*Ibid.*, p. 171.

[10]Brazeau, ''Language Differences and Occupational Experience,'' pp. 301-2.

[11]Keyfitz, ''Canadians and Canadiens,'' p. 174.

[12]Everett C. Hughes, *French Canada in Transition* (Chicago, 1943), p. 52.

[13]Paul-André Comeau, ''Acculturation ou assimilation: Technique d'analyse et tentative de mesure chez les franco-ontariens,'' *Canadian Journal of Political Science*, 2 (June, 1969), pp. 158-72.

[14]The working of these two processes is described in Jack Ladinsky, ''Careers of Lawyers, Law Practice, and Legal Institutions,'' *American Sociological Review*, 28 (February, 1963), pp. 47-54.

[15]*Ibid.*, pp. 51-4.

[16]Erwin O. Smigel, *The Wall Street Lawyer* (New York, 1964).

[17] Jerome Carlin, *Lawyers on Their Own* (New Brunswick, N.J., 1962).

[18] Charles Perrow, "A Framework For The Comparative Analysis of Organizations," *American Sociological Review*, 32 (April, 1967), pp. 194-208.

[19] Johnstone, *et. al., Survey of the Canadian Public Service*.

[20] *Ibid*.

[21] Adapted from Abraham Kaplan, "Power in Perspective" in Robert L. Kahn and Elise Boulding (eds.), *Power and Conflict in Organization* (New York, 1964), p. 25.

[22] Michel Crozier, *The Bureaucratic Phenomenon* (Chicago, 1964), p. 145.

[23] *Ibid*., p. 149.

[24] Harold L. Wilensky and Jack Ladinsky, "From Religious Community to Occupational Group: Structural Assimilation Among Professors, Lawyers, and Engineers," *American Sociological Review*, 32 (August, 1967), p. 545.

[25] *Ibid*., p. 558.

[26] As in Chapter 3, the seemingly deviant position of Agriculture can be explained by the fact that many of the Francophones feel markedly isolated from the mainstream of the department. These men have little desire to mix with the Anglophones and do not view their careers as subject to Anglophone control.

[27] Promotions in these settings are the result of "sponsored mobility" as the term is used in the ideal-type developed by Ralph H. Turner. The other type of mobility identified by Turner—"contest mobility"—seems to be dominant in routine settings as discussions in the text will indicate. See Ralph H. Turner, "Sponsored and Contest Mobility and the School System," *American Sociological Review*, 25 (December, 1960), pp. 855-67.

[28] Wilensky and Ladinsky, "From Religious Community to Occupational Group. . . ," p. 558-9.

Chapter Six

Summary and
Implications

I have examined two subsocieties. My focus was on the processes of separation and integration: how are members of the two separate subsocieties drawn together, and what is the nature of the relationship between the subsocieties? One source of societal integration is participation in the economy. Persons from diverse subsocieties are drawn into large public and private bureaucracies in order to obtain an income. Here they become acquainted with a wide range of persons and, unless the organization is controlled by a minority group, they are in regular contact with the norms, values, and beliefs of the dominant groups in the wider society. In addition, the pursuit of a career in these organizations tends to pull one away from one's subsociety and into communication with co-workers in the organization or with colleagues in the same occupation both inside and outside the organization.

It is obvious that the relations between persons from the two subsocieties will be greatly affected when one is both dominant in the wider society and in the organizations under study, while the other is an acknowledged minority. Therefore, the object of my study was to trace out the impact of majority and minority status on integration into economic organizations which were majority settings. I sought to find out how majority or minority status is related to four processes: the types of men from the two subsocieties who seek employment in large organizations, their motives for joining, their respective rates of social mobility, and, for minority men, the different rates of assimilation that various organizations and careers call forth. To explore these topics, I used Canadian findings about the Anglophone majority and Francophone minority pursuing careers at the middle-level of five departments in the federal administration.

In the Introduction, I asked four questions and advanced four hypotheses in reply. I can now review the questions and their answers. I will also identify some of the major determinants of the character of majority-minority relations, examine inter-group relations in several other societies in the light of my Canadian findings, and advance a set of testable propositions about the career mobility and assimilation of minority men in majority settings.

A. Review

Question 1.   How do majority and minority men differ in terms of social background, education, and work history, and do these factors affect entry to a bureaucratic career?
Hypothesis 1:   Minority men are drawn from a narrower geographic area, lower social origins, with less education and little other work experience.

A major point of difference between the majority (Anglophone) and minority (Francophone) groups is that the latter is almost completely (93 per cent) native-born. The majority group has been able to supplement its numbers from abroad, while relatively few foreigners have aligned themselves with the minority group. The minority is also more "provincial" in another sense of the word: nine out of ten are drawn from areas of minority concentration in the two central provinces of the country. Thus the middle-level minority personnel have rarely been born abroad and are drawn from a geographically-concentrated subsociety.

It is evident, also, that the minority subsociety contains at least two regional subcultures. One, the *Québecois*, is based in a region where Francophones control several major institutional complexes, in particular, an educational system which is able to provide complete training through university. The other regional sector of the minority subsociety is based in areas where Francophones lack power and must adjust to an educational system geared to majority culture. This sector includes the Franco-Ontarians. The upshot is that the *Québecois* are more likely to have the skills to enter professional and scientific careers than are the Franco-Ontarians.

Although these organizations have provided a white-collar position to large proportions of men from lowly origins in both subgroups—49 per cent of the minority and 44 per cent of the majority are of working class or farm origins—there is a tendency for the majority men to be of higher social origins. About 20 per cent of Francophones and 29 per cent of Anglophones are from the upper-middle class or above. Thus, both majority and minority groups contain several class subgroups, but the difference in the relative size of the class subgroups is not great. The impression given by these data is that access to higher education and the acquisition of expertise are of central importance in obtaining a middle-level post. However, since availability of education is a product of class position and a large proportion of intelligent offspring from disadvantaged families are unable to enter or stay in university, those from the lower end of the social scale are under-represented at the middle level.

Concerning the level and substance of the education possessed by minority and majority men, I find that persons in the minority group are less likely to have university degrees and if they have degrees, they are likely to be in arts, commerce, or law. The lack of university degrees is accounted for, in large measure, by the difficulties experienced by Franco-Ontarians in obtaining an education. Since the federal Public Service recruits heavily from this regional sector, the general level of education in the Francophone group is pulled down. As for educational specialization, the Anglophone majority reveals a strong emphasis on science and engineering training. Thus, the educational complexion of the two groups differs rather markedly with the majority group being more ''modern'' in its educational preparation. The prevalence in the federal administration of posts requiring a generalist education, however, ought not put the Francophones at too severe a disadvantage, at least in terms of educational specialization.

The minority men are more likely to enter federal employment directly after leaving school than are the majority men. Minority personnel seem more anxious to find a secure niche in a large organization. Majority men, by contrast, are more likely to have worked for several other employers before joining, and to have moved between geographic areas of the country. Interestingly, among those who worked outside the federal Public Service before joining, there is no gross difference between majority and minority personnel as to the amount of disruption in their work histories. Most appear to have made a fairly orderly sequence of job changes.

In sum, hypothesis 1 has been confirmed. The minority men are more likely to be native born, to be drawn from a limited geographic area, to be born into a social class near the bottom of the scale, to lack a university education, or, if university-trained, to have been in arts, commerce, or law; they are also prone to join the federal administration directly after leaving school. Some, and perhaps all of these factors, are conditioned by the fact that the minority group is composed of two regional subcultures: *Québecois* and Franco-Ontarians. These differences both between majority and minority men and within the minority group are fundamental in explaining attitudes to the workplace and the unfolding of careers.

Question 2.   Does taking a post in a majority setting have different meanings for majority and minority men?

Hypothesis 2.   Minority men are more prone to seek security and economic benefit in work while majority men are more motivated by the intrinsic interest of the job itself.

It is important to distinguish between two major clusters of motives that are associated with employment: the desire for challenging tasks and the opportunity to apply or learn skills (*work* factors) and the desire for security and the other rewards that employment provides (*benefit* factors). Minority men clearly sought after employment benefits more often than did majority men. The difference held up within career fields and among persons with little seniority.

The concern of Francophones with benefit matters is largely a reflection of the experiences of the Franco-Ontarian group. The latter had in its ranks 64 per cent who joined for benefit reasons. The *Québecois* expressed attitudes very similar to the Anglophone group. In fact, 40 per cent of both *Québecois* and all Anglophones cited benefit factors as their main reason for entering a federal department. Nearly half the *Québecois* were attracted to the middle-level by the character of the work going on there. The Franco-Ontarians seemed much more concerned about job security and staying in the local area.

In addition to the influence of ethnic-linguistic and regional cultures, occupational culture also affected attitudes about employment. In both linguistic groups, scientists and policy-makers place most emphasis on work factors, followed by semi-professionals, engineers, technicians, and lower administrators. Therefore, career type evokes marked and patterned differences, but its effects are tempered by ethnic-linguistic and regional cultures: Francophones are more prone to seek after benefits than Anglophones, and Franco-Ontarians are more benefit-oriented than the *Québecois*. By combining these three variables—career field, ethnic-linguistic origins, regional background—a quite exact understanding of the attitudes of men toward their work could be gained.

Minority men who are buffeted in their worklife before entering the federal administration are likely to view it as a haven of security. Majority men with the same experience are prone to view it as a workplace that offers further challenges. This reflects the market situation for minority and majority men. Since posts for Francophones seem to be harder to locate, a man whose employment suddenly ends has troubles. An Anglophone usually finds it easier to locate another job. Thus, Francophones and Anglophones with disorderly work histories view the Federal administration in different terms.

There are several work areas where majority-minority differences appear to be minimized. Among scientific researchers both Anglophones and Francophones seem dedicated to their discipline and the advancement of knowledge. The same applies to professional fields, like law, where a sojourn with the federal government is regarded by practitioners as good training for later work in the private sector. Few as they are in these work areas, the Francophones seem to be imbued with the same feelings as the majority men. Thus the hypothesis was generally confirmed with deviations being found among the *Québecois* and within certain work areas.

Question 3.   Are there differences in salary attainment and rate of career mobility for majority and minority men with similar qualifications?

Hypothesis 3. Majority men will have a significant salary advantage over their minority equivalents and will have a higher rate of career mobility.

The bureaucratic career, according to Weber and others, is a standardized, socially-recognized, vertical, and linear sequence of work roles; a sequence that is successfully traversed by persons who have advanced training and continue to demonstrate their competence over time. There is a certain amount of ambiguity in the discussions of bureaucratic careers by both theorists and bureaucrats as to the relative importance of seniority and achievement (as indicated by educational expertise). In addition, the place of "informal factors" such as the favouritism shown by superiors to juniors who are of the same ethnic, religious, or class backgrounds has often been noted in studies of career achievement. It is important, therefore, to unscramble the relative effects of seniority, education, age, and informal factors on the careers of minority and majority men.

In the first place, it appears that class origins are not a barrier to career attainment once one gains entry to these organizations. Six out of ten of the men in both the majority and minority groups have been able to attain a higher socio-economic position than that attained by their fathers. Education is the prime factor that has eliminated the influence of class origins. Those with advanced training, no matter what their class origins, are able to move upwards along these career routes.

Despite a tendency to join the federal administration early in their worklives, minority men also show a tendency to leave soon afterwards. Even with their headstart in these organizations, there are relatively few Francophones in the older age groups. They are concentrated not only in the younger age groups but also in technical, semi-professional, and administrative careers rather than in professional or scientific ones. These facts mean that it is crucial in comparing the career mobility of minority and majority men to control for age, education, and career type.

The hypothesis, with regard to salary attainment, is partially confirmed. When the educational levels and career types are divided into age groups, it is apparent that young minority men are doing as well or better in salary terms than their majority counterparts. It is in the older age groups that Francophones are at a disadvantage. The salary gap is quite pronounced between older majority and minority men with university degrees and between the older men in professional-scientific or administrative careers.

Age is directly related to salary attainment, but the majority men tend to receive almost twice as much for each passing year as do minority men. The effect of seniority on salary is slight, but majority men derive greater benefit from it than do minority men. For both minority and majority men, level and type of education is the single strongest determinant of salary level. It is of interest, however, that those in the ''Science-Engineering'' stream receive lower salaries than their counterparts in ''Arts.'' A related finding is that men in administrative careers fare better financially than men in professional-scientific or technical and semi-professional careers. When the combined effect of these several factors on salary level is assessed separately for minority and majority men it is possible to pinpoint the areas of greatest discrepancy: Francophones experience the greatest disadvantage compared to Anglophones among older unilingual administrators at all seniority levels with either a bachelors (E3) or postgraduate (E5) degree in an Arts field, and among older unilingual professional and scientific personnel with considerable seniority and possessing a bachelors (E3) or postgraduate (E5) degree in an Arts field. In salary, these older minority men are significantly behind their majority equivalents.

The explanation of why older majority men are ahead of older minority men presents difficult analytical problems. Since the regression results reflect only one point in time, it is necessary to examine historical factors that might account for the differentials. The factors examined are an alleged educational gap between older majority and minority men, higher and selective attrition from the ranks of the minority men, and informal discrimination.

Since the education of Francophones until recently was controlled by the Roman Catholic Church, it tended to be ''classical'' in nature, not technical or scientific. This fact, however, did not necessarily put Francophones at a disadvantage. The training they did receive was ideal preparation for administrative careers. In these "English" organizations, however, it was defined as inferior simply because it was French and Catholic. Although the substance of Francophone training was suitable for many careers in these organizations, the minority men were not given opportunities to prove their worth.

In the face of such obstacles, many left the federal administration when numerous, challenging posts to direct the economic and political restructuring of Quebec during the "Quiet Revolution" suddenly became available in the early 1960s. The career opportunities in Quebec seemed much better than those in the federal capital; the consequence was the departure of a great number of able and ambitious men from minority ranks. There does not appear to have been such a high rate of fallout, nor such selective attrition, from the ranks of the majority men during this period. Thus, there is some merit to the fallout explanation of the lower salaries of older minority men.

It is probable that the high fallout rate resulted, in part, then, from discrimination against Francophones in these "English" organizations. Further evidence of discrimination is found in the fact that Anglophones with bachelors degrees were able to command higher salaries than Francophones with postgraduate degrees. The regression results indicate that subtle, informal factors led to a growing disparity over time between majority and minority mens' salaries. Thus, career discrimination appears to be the primary factor accounting for the salary inequality and slower career mobility of minority men.

Question 4.   In what types of organizations and careers do minority men maintain the most viable ties to their ethnic-religious roots? Does employment in a majority setting mean the inevitable abandonment of the ethnic community off the job?

Hypothesis 4.   Minority men in routine and specialized work areas are able to maintain viable ties to their ethnic-religious roots.

At the middle-level of large, bureaucratic organizations internal promotions are the usual way of filling vacant positions.

Sponsorship for promotion, and the compatibility between senior and junior employees which sponsorship entails, often become prime factors in the promotion process. Those who lack sponsors or are felt by senior employees to be incompatible may find their upward climb slowed down. The Francophone minority, many of whom are conscious of personal difficulties in using the English language, are prone to feel that they are outsiders. Because of these difficulties with the English language and their interest in French Canadian culture, sociability with Anglophone superiors is hampered and the possibilities of sponsorship are lessened.

Clearly, advancement for minority men is closely related to structural assimilation, the entry into close personal relationships with members of the majority group. The need to assimilate varies, however, among Francophones and between work organizations. The Franco-Ontarians, early in life, become adept at living in an English environment. They also have to confront the fact that schooling is difficult to obtain, the local employment market is limited, and the French language and culture are given scant recognition in political or economic affairs in the province. A prime concern, then, is to obtain a secure job. In contrast, the *Québecois* tend to spend most of their pre-work lives in a French environment. They find schooling and employment fairly easy to obtain. Thus, when they come to select a workplace, the possibility of doing interesting work is uppermost in their minds. However, when they enter the middle-level of these federal organizations they are likely to have considerable trouble in using English.

The minority men tend to be concentrated in organizations of the routine rather than the creative type. Routine organizations are more accommodating to persons of diverse backgrounds, while creative organizations, which operate on the basis of employee autonomy and rich communication between co-workers, are less accommodative. As Hypothesis 4 predicted, routine or specialized work permits the minority man to continue his ethnic ties off the job, while creative work weakens them. Since Franco-Ontarians are concentrated in routine sectors, their ethnic ties remain strong. Minority men doing creative work—mainly *Québecois*—experience an erosion of ethnic ties. Thus, both personal choices and organization processes operate in determining who does or does not assimilate: men in search of secure employment who enter routine organizations face few threats to their ethnic roots while men who seek interesting work in creative organizations are subject to both a personal desire and organizational pressures to assimilate. Since most minority men employed in majority settings are in settings of the routine type, ethnic pluralism will continue to draw strength even from this group.

B. A Wider Perspective

How relevant are these Canadian findings for understanding relations between white majorities and minorities in majority settings in other societies? If majority-minority relations is the object of this study, are the findings so conditioned by peculiarities of Canadian history, the special status and legitimacy of the Francophone minority, the culture of the country, or the nature of its key institutions, that they cannot be generalized beyond its borders? The problem of generalizing from such findings has been pointed to by Robert Marsh:

> What is needed in sociology and anthropology is a systematic specification of which theories and propositions hold for all societies, which for only certain types of societies, and which for only individual societies.[1]

My treatment is more impressionistic than systematic, but it does indicate the start of a solution to this key analytical problem.

A formal outline of the analysis of the nature of majority-minority relations might look like the chart on page 172.[2]

The independent variables require brief comment. Societal type refers to membership in one of several categories of society, each category containing societies sharing common cultural and structural features. Various types have been identified, usually in terms of cultural tradition and level of economic development,e.g.,urban-industrial societies,underdeveloped countries, Caribbean societies, Communist states of Eastern Europe, Sub-Saharan Africa, Anglo-American societies. The second independent variable refers to the existence of agreement or

Outline for Analysis of Majority-Minority Relations

Independent Variables	Intervening Variables	Dependent Variable
1. Societal Type	1. Distinctive Societal Values	Majority-Minority Relations
2. Consensus or Conflict about Minority's Future	2. Legitimacy of Minority	
3. Dominant Institution in the Society: Economy or Polity	3. Degree of Difference in Culture or Language Between Majority and Minority	
	4. Historical Relationship Between Majority and Minority (Minority is Conquered, Autonomous, Original Dwellers, Early or Recent Arrivals)	
	5. Socio-Economic Position of Minority	

disagreement between dominant and subordinate groups as to the future position of the latter. There can be consensus or conflict about whether or not the minority will be assimilated or will retain its cultural autonomy, or whatever. The relative power in society of political or economic institutions is the third factor.[3] On the one hand are societies where political organs control and direct the economy, on the other are societies where economic units set the limits within which the polity acts. The former includes both Communist and non-Communist societies with a state-run economy or, at least, centralized and comprehensive economic planning. In the other situation, the private sector wields considerable power and the role of the polity is that of responding to or serving private interests and regulating rather than directing economic activity. Obviously, these three variables either singly or in combination are major determinants of the character of majority-minority relations. It will be important to "control for" or "hold constant" societal type (cultural traditions and level of economic development), conflict or consensus about minority's future, and relative power of polity or economy, in arriving at suggestive propositions.

Two studies have provided empirical verification of the importance of these variables. Both draw on the "cross-polity" files that have been developed by Banks and Textor and by

Russett and his associates.[4] Fishman examines one type of minority, the linguistic minority.[5] He compares societies which do or do not have linguistic minorities by using the data of Banks and Textor and discovers

> the well-known relationships between industrialization, urbanization, modernization, Westernization, Christianization, and homogenization that have been explicated by modern political philosophy, history, and sociology during the past century.[6]

Linguistically homogeneous societies are typically more developed economically, more advanced educationally, more urbanized and more stable politically than are societies containing linguistic minorities. When he controlled for level of economic development, Fishman found that heterogeneous societies revealed consistently higher levels of sectionalism, of political activity by anomic groups, and in general, higher levels of conflict. Among both "developed" and "underdeveloped" polities, the heterogeneous ones were less stable. Societal wealth, however, did reduce the level of sectionalism and instability. On the other hand, societies that were both poor and heterogeneous were highly prone to rancorous political conflict. Level of economic development, therefore, either reduces or aggravates the intensity of majority-minority relations.

Further specification of the relationships discussed by Fishman is provided by Inglehart and Woodward.[7] They, like Fishman, use data from Banks and Textor but employ a more refined breakdown of variables than he does. They use historical examples and statistical findings to show that linguistic pluralism is rarely translated into political separatism among both premodern and developed societies. It is in "transitional" or "developing" societies that the divisive force exerted by multiple language groups is greatest. In the pre-modern society the masses are generally inert and do not rally around any differentiating feature. At a high level of political or economic development the polity is better able to respond to collective demands and retain stability. In transitional societies, those which are linguistically heterogeneous are more likely than their homogeneous counterparts to show a history of political instability since World War II. The authors contend that transitional, heterogeneous societies are especially prone to instability because industrialism brings expectations of upward mobility and one linguistic group may find its route blocked by another. Where a dominant group gives preference in recruitment to those who speak its language, minority groups face the options of mobility through assimilation, immobility, or resistance. Many groups choose resistance, which may take the form of assaults on political authorities. The main point, however, is that level of economic development conditions the nature of majority-minority relations.

The effect of agreement or disagreement between majority and minority concerning the minority's future is so obviously important as a factor conditioning majority-minority relations that it really needs no further comment. The effect of having either political or economic institutions as the dominant ones in the society is also rather straightforward. Those societies in which the polity exercises strict control over the economy are also likely to display deliberate government intervention in the affairs of minority groups. This may take the form of exerting assimilation pressures, maintaining minorities as autonomous but subordinate, forcing them to migrate, or whatever. Where private economic organizations are dominant, minority groups are likely to have greater autonomy and be expected to decide on their own mode of adjustment to the surrounding society.

The implication of the foregoing discussion is that different readings on the three independent variables produce differences in majority-minority relations. In order to develop explanatory propositions it becomes imperative to examine a set of societies in which each society contains a similar reading on the three variables, then compare this set to other sets which vary from it along only one or two variables. The search for explanations of majority-minority relations, then, might begin with transitional Caribbean societies with a private-enterprise economy or with developed Anglo-American societies with a private-enterprise base. When one deals with a set of similar societies it also becomes possible to introduce into the explanation the intervening variables that I have listed above. Therefore, a fruitful analytic task is the study of a process or structure in the same institutional arena in several societies with the same gross characteristics.[8] The influence of the major independent variables and the manner in which their influence is conditioned by intervening variables can be specified. My focus on the Anglo-American democracies in the following paragraphs is an effort to move toward this goal. Basic aspects of Anglophone-Francophone relations in public organizations in Canada that I have reported earlier are used as a source of explanatory propositions that could apply to majority-minority relations in the public services of the other Anglo-American societies. The explanations, however plausible, are tentative and unproven; further comparative research is direly needed in order to provide a definitive test of the propositions.

An important first task is to indicate the characteristics that the four Anglo-American societies share in common, in addition to the traits they share as developed, urban-industrial societies.[9]

1. British political and legal traditions in the spheres of voting rights, individual freedoms, public debate, the rule of law, and the differentiation of legislative, executive, and judicial powers.
2. A "civic culture": citizens are frequently exposed to political issues, discuss politics, participate in political actions, and have access to a plurality of political groups.
3. A philosophy of activism, liberalism, pragmatism, and individualism.
4. Strong central government.
5. A clear Left-Right distinction on most domestic issues between (usually two) political parties.
6. An ethic of equality and a belief that most people in the society are "middle class."
7. A similar distribution of occupations in the labour force and of amounts of social mobility.

Since the four countries are similar in such significant ways, many social processes—including, perhaps, majority-minority relations in majority settings—can be expected to operate along similar lines. Any variation that is located can be traced to the limited set of intervening variables which do set the societies slightly apart from one another. Let me briefly indicate one limited difference between the four societies and how this could affect majority-minority relations in bureaucratic organizations, and, in particular, public bureaucracies. For example, it is clear that distinctive societal values in the four societies concerning equality and achievement inform the operations of their bureaucratic organizations.

Britain is one of the last societies with a secure aristocracy. It embodies an historic tradition that birth into a certain level of society brings with it a set of assets or liabilities that operate throughout one's life. Those born to high position can rightfully retain it. A tradition of elitism and deference to authority exists, although democracy has evolved in the political sphere and the value of personal achievement is now emphasized in economic and educational spheres. American society was born by the actions of people who rejected elitism. There was a strong emphasis on egalitarianism, on opening up elite positions to persons of demonstrated ability, and on developing a system of mass education that would allow the abilities of the whole population to be developed. There was a tradition that individuals or groups can challenge authority, often effectively. Australia had a slightly different value emphasis.[10] It, like the United States, was established as a British colony of independent small farmers. While this intent was largely realized in the United States, it was frustrated by geography in Australia. Farming proved difficult, but sheep-grazing proved to be easier. Sheep-grazing, however, required large holdings of land and a supply of hired hands. Thus, Australia was dominated initially by a rural gentry served by a class of propertyless men who furnished the labour supply. At the same time, the port cities of the country underwent rapid growth in size. When these city-dwellers wanted to get their own "piece of land" they found their way blocked by the landed gentry. Early on, then, the propertyless men in Australia learned the utility of class solidarity and collective effort; the institution of "mateship" dates from this period. An egalitarian ethic was matched with dependence on a strong central government to fight inequities, an effective labour party, and a powerful trade union movement. In stratification terms,

the span of the contemporary Australian class structure is still much narrower than that of the United States and the style of life of the middle class differs only slightly from that of the working class.[11]

Canada is a country of greater conservatism and elitism than is the United States or Australia, but it is not as elitist as Britain. Its early settlement was guided by bureaucratic organizations—fur companies, railroads, police forces—rather than by rugged individuals. Where the local marshall or sheriff who singlehandedly enforces law and order is the symbol of the American frontier, it is the "Mountie," a bureaucratic officer, who symbolizes the Canadian experience. In addition, at a formative stage in the country's history it received a large influx of people fleeing the American Revolution (the Loyalists) who imported a set of values focused on hierarchy, monarchy, and British attachment. Canadians came to disparage many of what they regarded as "excesses" of the American Revolution: mass education, the melting pot, a more equitable distribution of consumer goods, and so on. Robert Alford provides a handy summary of this discussion:

Thus, it might be said that America was born of revolution. Australia was born of revolutionaries without a revolution, Canada was born out of forces opposed to revolution, and modern Britain was not born at all, but has evolved under the guidance of the aristocracy to its present state.[12]

How do such national differences affect bureaucratic organizations and majority-minority relations within them? Again, my remarks must be brief and impressionistic.[13] There is some evidence that British organizations are markedly influenced by the stratification system from which they draw their members. Stephen Richardson, in his comparison of British and American merchant ships, notes that Britishers accept the authority of persons in higher positions and trust them not to misuse their authority.[14] Findings specifically about the British Public Service indicate that there is a tendency for the top positions to be held by men with the "superior" background of an Oxford or Cambridge education.[15] The British system contains an "Administrative Class" of such men whose origins are in the upper reaches of the stratification system. There is a tendency to ensure the smooth operation of organizations by recruiting men for management positions who traditionally are accorded deference and respect. American orgnizations are prone to play down status differences, to depend on specialized competence in assigning men to positions of authority, and to operate with a set of impersonal rules that protect against abuses of power. Richardson's study of American ships clearly indicates this. Where British organizations are managed by men of high social origins with generalist training, American organizations prefer candidates with expertise and practical experience. In public organizations in the United States positions at every level of the organization are open to the outsider with expertise.

> Efforts to create a senior civil service with some but not all of the characteristics of the British administrative class have so far met with resistance as contrary to the spirit and operating needs of the American public service.[16]

There is an emphasis in American society on awarding elite posts to persons who have attained advanced training and who then demonstrate their worth in an open contest with others who possess the same training.[17]

A major study has indicated that the emphasis in the United States on educational attainment and personal achievement is an integral part of the "melting pot" process.[18] The Duncans used data from a national sample of American-born, non-Negro males ages 25 to 64 in 1962. They located fairly substantial differences between national-origin groups in terms of educational and occupational attainment but argue against the existence of pervasive discrimination on purely ethnic grounds. The paper compared the native-born whose fathers were also native-born to those whose fathers had been born in various foreign countries. One basic finding was that "the rather sharp differentials in formal schooling by nationality that obtained in the parental generation did not persist among their native sons, who assimilated the American norms of school attendance."[19] Furthermore, when men with similar social origins (similar father's education and occupation) and similar educational attainment but differing in national origins are compared in terms of occupational achievement, there are no significant differences between national groups. The only major groups continuing to operate with a modest handicap are the Italian-Americans and Latin-Americans. Among those achieving increasingly greater occupational success are the Irish, the Germans, the Russians, and men whose origins trace to nations of northwest Europe other than Ireland and Germany. The implication of these findings is that since white minority groups with equal levels of education receive equal treatment in the economy, the further equalization of educational opportunity will largely eliminate current nationality-group differences.[20]

With reference to the American federal Public Service, W. Lloyd Warner and his colleagues[21] report on the birthplaces of civilian federal executives. Well over half of those surveyed (58 per cent) in 1959 were "old American": the person, his father, and his grandfather had been born in the United States. Only 4 per cent were foreign born but a fifth had fathers who were born abroad. The social origins of the men whose fathers had been born abroad were compared to the origins of the old Americans. It was found that the sons of immigrants were more likely to have risen from humble origins than were the offspring of old American families. The authors conclude that vertical occupational mobility is greater for the sons of the foreign born who enter the federal Public Service than for the offspring of persons who have been established in American society for longer periods of time. This provides them with evidence that " 'the American dream' and the myth of the melting pot do have some validity for the sons of immigrant fathers"[22] at least in the federal executive.

The Australians, like the Americans, focus on individual achievement but play down the necessity of expert training. "Until recently a university education was not required for most managerial occupations nor for higher civil service position."[23] University training was regarded as just another status distinction, and Australians refuse to respect status differences. The Commonwealth Public Service was created as a closed-system open only to youths who would make it a lifetime career.[24] Promotion to higher positions was to be strictly from within the organization. The idea that persons with university degrees or expert training could be parachuted into the middle or upper ranks was shunned, and the British tradition of creating an Administrative Class avoided. In recent years, there has been a greater tendency to bring in outside experts and to accommodate university graduates, but the basic principle of a closed system with entry at the bottom has not been abandoned.

Although the dominant tone of Australian life is that of egalitarianism and loyalty to one's mates, there is an undercurrent of intolerance to ethnic minorities and a sense of the superiority of British virtues.[25] The harsh treatment of the aboriginal natives and Asian migrants which led to the White Australian Policy is one manifestation of this tendency. Up until the period just after the Second World War, the prevailing sentiment was against non-British immigration. Although white, non-British immigrants are now generally tolerated and few verbal or physical assaults on minority persons occur, recent opinion surveys reveal no trend toward cultural pluralism.[26] Newcomers are expected to acquire the English language and British ways soon after their arrival. Since about 80 per cent of the Australian population is of British ethnic origin, the expectation of Anglo-conformity has been felt to be natural.[27]

Although minority men in Australia face a variety of handicaps, the handicaps appear to be fairly equally distributed among the different minorities. Lieberson has compared the adaptation of "old" immigrant groups (mainly northwestern Europeans from Belgium, France, Germany, Netherlands, and Sweden, among others) to the "new" groups that have recently begun to reach Australia in large numbers (mainly southern Europeans from Greece, Hungary, Italy, Malta, and Poland, among others).[28] His aim is to test the hypothesis that the old groups from northern and western Europe

have higher rates of assimilation, cause fewer social problems, are of hardier stock, and merge more rapidly with the native population than do immigrants from other areas of Europe.[29]

The hypothesis is not supported. He found that there are grounds to suppose that the "new" groups are adapting and will adapt along the same lines as the "old" groups. Nevertheless, although minority groups receive similar treatment, other research indicates there are still marked socio-economic differentials between minority groups and the British-Australian majority. Studies by Zubrzycki[30] reveal the relative scarcity of minority men in the higher circles of the economy and polity. Public authorities, professional fields, and financial affairs, more so than other areas, are the special preserves of the native Australians and British-born immigrants. There is some evidence, then, that despite Australia's ethic of equality, minority men in Australia experience some difficulties in adjusting to the "British" aspects of Australian society.

The foregoing has indicated that Britain, United States, and Australia, despite their basic similarity, do reveal distinctive values concerning equality and achievement. These value emphases influence the inner workings of complex organizations within each society, in particular conditioning the relations between majority and minority men. It is now possible to bring in my own findings about Canada and advance several testable propositions about white majority-minority relations in majority settings in the four countries. The propositions will be stated in terms of work settings in the public sector, although they likely are applicable to settings in the private sector as well.

My study reveals that minority men are prone to seek secure employment. In the course of their careers the cumulative effect of informal discrimination is likely to slow up their rate of upward career mobility in comparison to majority men. This is, in part, because they have to contend with the sponsorship system in order to obtain promotions in majority settings. This system emphasizes sociability between superiors and their juniors, particularly in creative organizations. The pressures to assimilate are also considerable. Routine organizations place more emphasis on regular performance and exert less pressure toward assimilation. The top level of even routine organizations, however, is a place of marked assimilation pressure. The following are the implications of these facts for the career mobility and rate of assimilation of minority men in the majority settings of the four Anglo-American democracies, also taking into account their distinctive societal values.

(1) White minorities in Britain, more so than in the other three societies, confront a more rigid and secure set of bureaucratic

relations than do white minorities in the other Anglo-American states. Upward career mobility is relatively slow. However, minority men who obtain a ''proper'' education experience fewer blockages than those who do not obtain one. Pressures to assimilate are great throughout both creative and routine organizations.

(2) Canadian organizations are less rigid than those in Britain, but as my discussion in Chapter Two indicates, middle and top management tend to be drawn from the upper reaches of the class system and to be of a generalist bent. Canadian minorities are likely to confront difficulties in a sponsorship system which caters to these types of men although the difficulties are not as formidable as in Britain. Assimilation pressures are great on those minority men who do aspire to move up in creative organizations or into the top level of routine organizations, but the national emphasis on a cultural mosaic reduces the pressures on minority men at the middle level of routine organizations.

(3) Australia places more emphasis on equality and the rewarding of personal achievement than does either Britain or Canada. Upward career mobility is the reward for individual effort, not an automatic privilege for those who possess a university degree. However, minority men must carve out a career against a background of mild intolerance of ethnic-linguistic differences. This likely slows the career mobility of minority men in comparison to their majority equivalents, but they probably fare better in Australia than in Canada or Britain. In terms of assimilation, the pressure would be as great in Australia as in Britain.

(4) Minority men who acquire a specialist education and are willing to compete for advancement have more opportunities in the United States than in the other three societies. The key to success is the acquisition of education, although even without special training white minority men are likely to face fewer handicaps. The personal cost is assimilation for those in creative organizations or who enter the top of routine ones. The American melting pot operates effectively, although at the middle level of routine organizations a minority identity could be preserved. Canada, however, offers more opportunity than the United States for the preservation of a minority identity in majority settings.

In summary, I would predict that the upward career mobility of minority men in majority settings would be greatest in the United States, followed by Australia, Canada, Britain. Pressures to assimilate would be considerable in creative organizations and at the top level of routine organizations in all countries. However, at the middle level of routine organizations, assimilation would be least in Canada, but increasingly prevalent in the United States, Australia, and Britain.

This suggests some of the ways in which minority-majority relations in majority settings might differ in four similar countries. However, the main point of the discussion should not be lost: the form and direction of minority-majority relations can be expected to be quite similar in the Anglo-American democracies; those slight differences in form that are found can be directly traced to one of the few factors, such as distinctive values concerning equality and achievement, which show variation between the four societies. Thus, a sociological study of Francophones and Anglophones in Canada leads to propositions that can be applied to an understanding of intergroup relations beyond the borders of one society.

Notes

[1]Robert M. Marsh, *Comparative Sociology* (New York, 1967), p. vii.

[2]The scheme is adapted from R. A. Schermerhorn, *Comparative Ethnic Relations* (New York, 1970). Several of the intervening variables are also discussed in Hubert M. Blalock, Jr., *Toward a Theory of Minority-Group Relations* (New York, 1967).

[3]Schermerhorn, *Comparative Ethnic Relations*, pp. 176-87.

[4]Arthur S. Banks and Robert B. Textor, *A Cross-Polity Survey*, (Cambridge, Mass., 1965); Bruce M. Russett, *et. al.*, *World Handbook of Political and Social Indicators* (New Haven, 1964).

[5]Joshua A. Fishman, "Some Contrasts Between Linguistically Homogeneous and Linguistically Heterogeneous Polities," *Sociological Inquiry*, 36 (Spring, 1966), pp. 146-58.

[6]*Ibid.*, p. 152.

[7]Ronald F. Inglehart and Margaret Woodward, "Language Conflicts and Political Community," *Comparative Studies in Society and History*, 10 (October, 1967), pp. 27-45.

[8]Ivan Vallier, "Empirical Comparisons of Social Structure: Leads and Lags" in Ivan Vallier (ed.), *Comparative Methods in Sociology: Essays on Trends and Applications* (Berkeley, Calif., 1971).

[9]The similarities between the four societies are most fully treated in Seymour Martin Lipset's *The First New Nation, The United States in Historical and Comparative Perspective* (New York, 1963) and "The Value Patterns of Democracy: A Case Study in Comparative Analysis," *American Sociological Review*, 28 (August, 1963), pp. 515-31, and in Robert R. Alford, *Party and Society, The Anglo-American Democracies* (Chicago, 1963).

[10]The following discussion of Australia is derived from Kurt B. Mayer, "Social Stratification in Two Equalitarian Societies: Australia and the United States," *Social Research*, 31 (Winter, 1964), pp. 435-65.

[11]Mayer, "Social Stratification in Two Equalitarian Societies," p. 465.

[12]Alford, *Party and Society*, p. 31.

[13]I am guided in my comments by Crozier's analysis of how French culture is reflected in the operations of public and private bureaucracies in France. See Michel Crozier, *The Bureaucratic Phenomenon* (Chicago, 1963), Chaps. 8 and 9.

[14]Stephen A. Richardson, "Organizational Contrasts on British and American Ships," *Administrative Science Quarterly*, 1 (September, 1956), pp. 189-207.

[15]R. K. Kelsall, *Higher Civil Servants in Britain* (London, 1956) and R. K. Kelsall, "The Social Background of the Higher Civil Service" in William A. Robson, editor, *The Civil Service in Britain and France* (London, 1956), pp. 151-60.

[16]Ferrel Heady, *Public Administration: A Comparative Perspective*, (Englewood Cliffs, N.J., 1966), p. 47.

[17]A comparison of American and British education brings this out clearly. See Ralph H. Turner, "Sponsored and Contest Mobility and the School System," *American Sociological Review*, 25 (December, 1960), pp. 855-67.

[18]Beverly Duncan and Otis Dudley Duncan, "Minorities and the Process of Stratification," *American Sociological Review*, 33 (June, 1968), pp. 356-64.

[19]*Ibid.*, p. 360.

[20]Further evidence of the decline in socio-economic differences between white ethnic groups, particularly between those that are mainly Protestant and those that are mainly Catholic, is provided by Charles H. Anderson, *White Protestant Americans: From National*

Origins to Religious Group (Englewood Cliffs, N.J., 1970), Chap. 11.

[21]W. Lloyd Warner, *et. al.*, *The American Federal Executive* (New Haven, 1963).

[22]*Ibid.*, p. 64.

[23]Mayer, "Social Stratification in Two Equalitarian Societies," p. 451.

[24]Howard A. Scarrow, *The Higher Public Service of the Commonwealth of Australia* (Durham, N.C., 1957), Chap. 4.

[25]Richard N. Rosencrance, "The Radical Culture of Australia" in Louis Hartz, *The Founding of New Societies* (New York, 1964), pp. 275-318, and Ronald Taft, *From Stranger to Citizen* (London, 1966).

[26]Taft, *From Stranger to Citizen*, pp. 21-3.

[27]Charles Price, "Southern Europeans in Australia: Problems of Assimilation," *International Migration Review*, 2 (Summer, 1968), pp. 3-26.

[28]Stanley Lieberson, "The Old-New Distinction and Immigrants in Australia," *American Sociological Review*, 28 (August, 1963), p. 550-65.

[29]*Ibid.*, p. 533 (italics removed).

[30]Jerry Zubrzycki, *Immigrants in Australia* (Melbourne, 1960), and Jerzy Zubrzycki, "Some Aspects of Structural Assimilation of Immigrants in Australia," *International Migration*, 6 (1968), pp. 102-10.

Postscript: Eight Years Later

Since 1965-66, when the respondents on which this book is based were first contacted, there has been a flurry of activity in and about the Federal Public Service aimed at improving the position of the French language and Francophone personnel. Large numbers of Anglophone personnel have been enrolled in French-language courses. Senior executives have been given the opportunity for total immersion in the other culture. The appointments of Francophones to senior positions have received wide publicity, while the appointments of a number of French-Canadian cabinet ministers have further contributed to a general feeling that things are changing in the federal administration. Conventional wisdom, especially in civil service circles in Ottawa, has been that the Francophone has better chances for promotion.

In 1973-74, through the good offices of Dr. Pierre Coulombe of the Treasury Board, I was able to test some aspects of this conventional wisdom, by locating the original respondents and obtaining some limited information about their subsequent careers. Those who had left government employment were identified and I was given the current position and salary range[1] of those who remained.

TABLE P.1

Comparisons of 1965 and 1973 Salaries for Francophones and Anglophones by Age Group.

Age in 1965	Percent Increase		Absolute Increase	
	Francophones	Anglophones	Francophones	Anglophones
25-29	159.77	194.67	10734.39	14421.93
30-34	132.66	139.41	11083.61	12216.89
35-39	118.08	133.97	10091.21	12308.48
40-45	106.85	111.29	9218.56	10719.68

[1]The Public Service Commission would not release the exact salary of the respondent but provided a salary range for his position within which his current salary fell. I used the mean of the salary range as each person's salary.

Salary Differences

The new bicultural emphasis in the Public Service would lead us to expect a higher rate of salary increase for Francophone personnel. The findings presented in Table P.1 reveal that these expectations are unfounded. In every age group, the percentage salary increase for Anglophones is higher.

It appears, then, that the Anglophone-Francophone salary gap for these middle-level men has not narrowed. This finding is at odds with the pattern of salary differences discovered by Lanphier and Morris[2] who compared 1961 census results with a 1968 national survey. They found a diminution in salary differences in the upper end of the occupational scale (professional, managerial and sales workers), the very type of personnel with which I am concerned.

The most important point to note in this table is the widening of the gap between Anglophone and Francophone personnel in the youngest age group. In the 1965 study these men were on a relatively equal footing and there was the possibility that this was the beginning of a new trend toward equality. Almost ten years later, with these men in an older age bracket, the Anglophones have received greater salary benefit.[3]

Changes in Work Setting

With a bicultural emphasis it was hoped that Francophones would be more likely to make public service a lifetime career and to move more freely between departments. As Table P. 2 shows, however, Francophones are more likely than Anglophones to leave their government careers. Since 1965, 22 per

[2]C. M. Lanphier and R. N. Morris, "Structural Aspects of Differences in Income between Anglophones and Francophones," *The Canadian Review of Sociology and Anthropology,* Vol. 11, No. 1 (Feb. 1974), 53-66.

[3]Some of the Anglophone advantage may be a result of the fact that this group contains a slightly higher proportion of degree holders, but educational training prior to entry into the Public Service should not continue, in 1973, to carry such a strong influence.

cent of Francophones, as opposed to 15 per cent of Anglophones have quit their jobs in the public service. The pattern of higher Francophone attrition holds true for every department. Conversely, there is a greater tendency for Anglophones in every department to remain in the same work setting over this period. These findings are surprising in light of the earlier result which indicated the Francophones were more likely to seek security of employment.

Interpretation

Earlier in this book (Chapter 6) and in an article with Byron Spencer,[4] I speculated on some of the reasons for the disadvantaged position of Francophones. These new data permit further refinement of the earlier explanations for the lower Francophone salaries. One theory held that educational gaps existed, and that Francophones' less "modern" education would explain their lower salary levels. A second possibility was that able and educated Francophones had left the public service at a higher than normal rate, leaving behind the less able and educated, who would naturally receive lower salaries. The third, and most likely, explanation was that discrimination accounted for the salary disadvantage for Francophones.

The educational gap was primarily a phenomenon of the 1940's and 50's, and it shows up in the lower salaries of older minority men. Since that time the Quiet Revolution in Quebec and the emphasis on modernism in Francophone communities outside Quebec has closed the educational gap. Younger Francophones now receive educations quite similar to their Anglophone counterparts. This had become evident as early as 1965 in the salary equality between younger members of the two linguistic groups with like characteristics. These younger Francophones who were the chief beneficiaries of the revamped educational system ought to have continued to receive equal salary treatment, but it is precisely these younger men, as Table

[4]Christopher Beattie and Byron G. Spencer, "Career Attainment in Canadian Bureaucracies: Unscrambling the Effects of Age, Seniority, Education, and Ethnolinguistic Factors on Salary," *American Journal of Sociology*, Vol. 77, No. 3 (Nov. 1971), pp. 472-490.

TABLE P.2

Work Settings in 1973 of those Francophones and Anglophones who were at the Middle Level of Five Departments in the Canadian Public Service in 1965.

	Same Setting	Different Setting Within Public Service	Left Public Service	N*
State				
Francophone	71%	8%	21%	24
Anglophone	79%	7%	14%	29
Finance				
Francophone	33%	33%	33%	6
Anglophone	43%	39%	18%	28
Agriculture				
Francophone	68%	11%	21%	28
Anglophone	73%	14%	14%	37
Public Works				
Francophone	52%	22%	26%	27
Anglophone	71%	13%	16%	31
Revenue				
Francophone	63%	20%	17%	30
Anglophone	73%	12%	15%	33
Total				
Francophone	62%	17%	22%	115
Anglophone	68%	17%	15%	158

P. 1 has shown, who have experienced the most marked disadvantage.

As for the fallout explanation, it has already been found that the Francophones have a higher attrition rate than the Anglophones: but are those who leave the most educated and able? An analysis of the Francophone drop-outs showed that those with University degrees were over-represented and those without degrees were under-represented. However, an analysis of the Anglophones showed a similar, though slightly weaker trend. A comparison of Figure P. 1 with Figure 2.5 shows that the main difference among the drop-outs, as compared to the total sample, is that a larger proportion of Anglophones with some University dropped out. Thus, while it is shown that Francophones had a slightly higher drop-out rate, and that among the drop-outs the proportion of graduates was somewhat higher, the relative educational inferiority of the remaining

FIGURE P.1

Level of Education of Francophone and Anglophone Drop-outs.

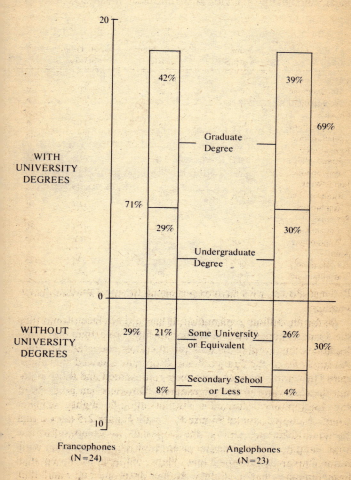

Francophones
(N=24)

Anglophones
(N=23)

group is not sufficient to explain its significant salary disadvantages.

Finally, we turn to the explanation of the salary gap in terms of career discrimination. That younger Francophones have fared worse than their Anglophone equivalents since 1965 indicates that those Francophones who ought to have the most potential have not received benefits equal to their Anglophone counterparts. On the other hand, the older Francophone personnel, who were especially disadvantaged in 1965, have been receiving increases close to those of their Anglophone counterparts.

With these recent findings I can conclude with a paraphrase of what I earlier stated in Chapter Four. There continues to be a greater fallout from the ranks of the Francophones, but it is not so top-heavy with the highly educated as to lower seriously the level of Francophone talent left behind. Career discrimination still appears to operate, although with the more equal treatment for older Francophone employees, it seems to have been reduced. It does seem, therefore, that there has been a slight reduction in discriminatory practices.

Appendix I
The Weighting Process

Quantitative results reported in tables or the text for either "All Anglophones" or the "Total Middle Level" have been weighted. The purpose of this appendix is to explain why and how this was done.

In the case of Anglophones, we drew five samples from five departments. The samples varied in size from 28 cases to 38 cases. However, the departmental populations from which they were drawn showed a much larger variation: from 48 to 279 persons. In fact, one sample contained about 58 per cent of the departmental population while another contained about 13 per cent. Since some samples represented or "stood for" a large number of people while others represented a small population, it was decided that an accurate representation of the Anglophone Middle Level could only be arrived at by giving extra weight to the samples which represented large populations and devaluing those samples which represented small populations. A weighting factor was derived for each department by using the following formula:

$$\text{Weighting Factor} = \frac{(\text{Departmental population}) (\text{Total Anglophone sample: 168})}{(\text{Departmental sample}) (\text{Total Anglophone population: 768})}$$

The weighting factor was easily obtained by inserting the size of the departmental population and sample into the formula. These are the results:

Department	Sample	Population	Weighting Factor
Finance	28	48	.38
Agriculture	37	279	1.65
National Revenue (Taxation)	33	154	1.02
Public Works	32	173	1.19
Secretary of State	38	114	.66
Total	168	768	

These factors were applied to the numerical distribution within each departmental sample of the chosen variable. The numerical result of each category of the variable was adjusted up or down in each department, depending on the weighting factor. It was then possible to add the five adjusted results for each category and thus obtain a weighted numerical distribution for the combined samples. A brief example will explain the process.

Within each departmental sample, each unweighted category of the variable "Ethnic Origin" is multiplied by the proper weighting factor to give a weighted result. The new distribution for the Anglophone Middle Level is obtained by adding the five new figures. Note that 168 remains the case base not only for the unweighted total (119 + 28 + 21) but also for the weighted total (123 + 27 + 18). The new weighted distribution is the one that would be used to calculate the results reported for "All Anglophones" in the tables or text.

The same logic was applied in arriving at results for the "Total Middle Level." Each of the five departments studied contained many more Anglophones than Francophones. It will be recalled that in four of five departments every available Francophone was contacted. On the Anglophone side, only a sample of persons was studied in each department. Therefore, the Anglophone samples represent a large population while the Francophone results are almost a complete count. When the Anglophone and Francophone results are combined in order to obtain findings about the whole middle level, it is necessary to give extra weight to the Anglophone results. The weighting factors obtained were 1.47 for the Anglophones and .38 for the Francophones. As above, these factors were applied to the numerical distribution of the chosen variable. The distributions used were the "All Francophones" (N:128) one and the weighted results for "All Anglophones" (N:168). Again, the case base of 296 remained for the weighted distribution. This new distribution was used to obtain findings for the "Total Middle Level."

	British		European		Other	
Department and Weighting Factor	Unweighted	Weighted	Unweighted	Weighted	Unweighted	Weighted
Finance (.38)	20	7.6	3	1.2	5	1.9
Agriculture (1.65)	28	46.2	6	9.9	3	5.0
National Revenue (1.02) (Taxation)	29	29.6	1	1.0	3	3.0
Public Works (1.19)	23	27.4	6	7.2	3	3.6
Secretary of State (.66)	19	12.5	12	7.9	7	4.7
Total	119	123.3	28	27.2	21	18.2

Chosen Variable: Ethnic Origin

Appendix 2

Descriptions of
Selected Variables

This Appendix describes several variables in more detail than could be provided in the text. To be specific, two variables which are both introduced for the first time in Chapter Two are treated here: "Social Class Background" and "Incidence of Disorderly Job-Switching."

A. Social Class Background

The determination of the class origins of each respondent was made by the use of answers given to four questions in the questionnaire concerning the respondent's father. The questions used are numbers 11, 12, 13, and 14, which refer respectively to father's occupation, major employer, income, and level of education. Given the limited nature of this data, only a rough four-class scale was used. The guidelines given to the coders are supplied below. The coders were also instructed that they were to treat the class system as it was 20-40 yeas ago and not to impose standards from the present day. Difficult cases were discussed by the coders and the study director so that general agreement as to classification procedures could be arrived at.

1. Upper and Upper-Middle Class
Includes mainly professional and managerial occupations. Includes also anyone who has a university degree. But excludes (1) professionals who are teachers or ministers without a university degree, and (2) managers without university attendance who earned $3,000 a year or under. The latter two categories are placed in the lower-middle class.

2. Lower-Middle Class
Includes mainly white-collar clerical and sales persons. Usu-

ally they had either some high school or completed high school, but did not complete university. Includes also self-employed skilled tradesmen who earned $3,000 or more a year.

3. Working Class

Includes mainly skilled tradesmen, semi-skilled tradesmen, and labourers.

4. Farmers

Includes farm owners, farm tenants, and farm labourers.

B. Incidence of Disorderly Job-Switching

This variable refers only to the respondent's work history outside the federal Public Service. "Outside," for nearly all, means their work history prior to joining the federal administration. But for a few persons it may include experiences after leaving a federal post and before rejoining.

In examining the outside work history, the focus was on the degree of stability of employment the person had experienced. The research of Harold L. Wilensky[1] suggested that this was an important dimension to consider. In the interview, the respondents were asked to review, under a set of headings, the sequence of work settings and jobs in which they had been before joining the Public Service. The question and the headings are given in the interview schedule (Beattie *et. al.,* App. IV, Que. 21). Note that in the actual interview schedule the headings were spread out along the top of a large sheet and the interviewer had plenty of room to write in the relevant details about every setting or job change.

An effort was made to record both changes of work setting or job. A change of work setting included not only shifts between one employer and another, but also shifts into and out of self-employment. Job changes could include not only changes from one occupation to another as one shifted between work settings,

---

[1] Harold L. Wilensky, "Orderly Careers and Social Participation: The Impact of Work History on Social Integration in the Middle Mass," *American Sociological Review*, 26 (August, 1961), pp. 521-39.

but also a significant change in duties within a single work setting. Since there was a certain amount of unevenness between interviewers in recording such changes, only a rough scoring of the orderliness or disorderliness of the work history was attempted. It was assumed that there were three types of moves that could occur in changes of setting or job, each type of move involving a different degree of discontinuity. In identifying and scoring each move, the coder was instructed to focus on the extent to which the previous post contributed to or was continuous with the present position. These were the three types of moves.

1. Horizontal Moves

These are situations where the subject is the practitioner of some profession or craft or trade and he continues to apply his profession or trade while making moves within or between settings. Best examples here are reporters, announcers, architects and teachers. Other professionals like accountants, lawyers, and engineers often make horizontal moves, but not always, since they at times shift into pure administration. The basic question to ask in verifying a Horizontal or H-Move is the following: Is the respondent doing roughly the same duties —i.e., applying the same learned skills or training—in present position A as in former position B?

2. Same-Area Moves

Again we focus on the contribution which job B has for job A. A Same-Area move involves one where the occupational duties have changed, but there is still some link between the two positions. In effect what the respondent has learned in position B helps him in new position A, or at least position B involves working in the same subject area, such as taxation or real estate, or chemistry. An example of a SA-Move would be a high school chemistry teacher who takes up a post as a chemist in private industry.

3. Clean Breaks

These moves are presumed to be the most disruptive, for they involve little or no continuity between positions. Generally the respondent moves into a wholly new institutional sphere or takes up completely different duties. An example of a CB-Move is the radio announcer who becomes a lumber salesman or the clerk who quits his job and returns to school, then becomes an engineer.

When the coding was done, it was possible to arrive at a score for the orderliness-disorderliness of the respondent's work history. The total number of each type of move was derived, then the number of H-Moves were multiplied by one, the number of SA-Moves by two, and the number of CB-Moves by three. The three scores were added to give a single, overall total.

It was obvious, however, that these scores had different meanings depending on the length of time the person had spent in outside employment. If the same score was given to two persons and one had a short work history and the other a lengthy one, this indicated that the person with the lengthy history had spaced out his moves over a longer period—a more stable pattern. A person who moved frequently over a short period was felt to display more disorderliness. In short, it was important to adjust the orderliness-disorderliness score for one's length of outside employment. The following indicates the combinations of disorder score and length of outside employment which composed the various categories of the variable.

Category	Disorder Score	Years of Outside Employment
Direct Entry	0	0
Orderly	1-3	4 and up
Slight Disorder	1-3	1-3
	4-7	4 and up
Medium Disorder	4-7	1-3
	8 and up	9 and up
High Disorder	8 and up	1-8

The results derived from this scheme are presented in Table 2.15.

Appendix 3

Results of the Multiple Regression Analysis

This appendix contains four tables which present the detailed results of the analysis reported on in Chapter 4. It will be recalled that the analysis employed the following variables: salary, age, years of service, career type, education, and ethno-linguistic category. Three of these variables—salary, age, and years of service—are continuous and posed no major analytic difficulties. The remaining variables, however, were discrete (nominal) and required special treatment. Each category of these latter variables was treated as a "dummy" variable which varied from 0 (present) to 1 (absent). This meant that a relationship between a category of a discrete variable and the continuous variables could be ascertained. In addition, the technique requires that the relations between "dummy" and continuous variables, e.g., between career type and salary, be by comparison. In each of the discrete variables one category is constrained to zero—E3, CT-Admin, FR-B—and the other categories are compared to the constrained one. Thus the effect of education on salary is indicated as a sum of money that would be either added or subtracted to one's salary. The sum indicated is based on the premise that E3 brings no money. Thus, E1 and E2, lower levels of education than E3, bring a salary decrease while E5, a higher level of education, generally brings a sum to be added. In this way the effect of different types and levels of education on salary is ascertained. It is the strategy of using "dummy" variables and constraining certain "dummy" variables to zero which lies behind the equations reported in Chapter 4.

The equations were also used to estimate salaries for men possessing different combinations of characteristics. The salary levels were estimated for all combinations of three ages (25, 35, 45), six education groups, three career types, and three seniority levels (5, 10, and 15 years of service). However, not all of these

162 combinations seemed plausible. The following were dropped out: (1) CT-P&S with E1 or E2, (2) CT-TECH with E5 or E6, and (3) age 25 with long years of service (10 or 15 years). The remaining 98 combinations are laid out in Table A7.1. Here "0" indicates a characteristic is absent and "1" that it is present. Combination 1, for instance, is a person 25 years old with an E4 level of education in a professional or scientific career and with 5 years of government service. Note that the constrained categories (E3 or CT-Admin) are considered as being present when the other education or career-type categories are all indicated as being absent. In combination 49, for instance, E3 is considered as being present since all the other education categories are absent.

Table A7.2 gives the salary estimates for all 98 combinations of characteristics, but, in addition, broken down into six ethno-linguistic groups: All Francophones, Unilingual Francophones, Bilingual Francophones, All Anglophones, Unilingual Anglophones, and Bilingual Anglophones. It is then possible to locate salary differentials between Francophones and Anglophones with the same combination of characteristics. This is done in Table A7.3, which indicates the results when All Anglophones are subtracted from All Francophones, Unilingual Anglophones from Unilingual Francophones, and Bilingual Anglophones from Bilingual Francophones.

The t-score was used to indicate whether or not the salary differentials are significant. The t-score is the ratio of the salary differential to its standard error. Using a 5% level of significance, a t-score larger than 1.645 indicates that a salary differential is significant. The t-scores are given in Table A7-4.

TABLE A7-1

All Possible Combinations of Age, Education, Career Type, and Years of Service*

	1	2	3	4	5	6	7	8	9	10	11	12	13	14	15	16	17	18	19	20	21
Age	25.	35.	45.	25.	35.	45.	25.	35.	45.	25.	35.	45.	25.	35.	45.	25.	35.	45.	25.	35.	45.
E 1	0.	1.	0.	1.	1.	1.	0.	0.	0.	0.	0.	0.	0.	0.	1.	0.	0.	0.	0.	0.	0.
E 2	1.	0.	0.	0.	0.	0.	0.	0.	0.	0.	0.	0.	0.	0.	0.	0.	0.	0.	0.	0.	0.
E 4	0.	0.	1.	0.	0.	0.	0.	0.	0.	0.	0.	1.	0.	0.	0.	0.	0.	0.	0.	0.	0.
E 5	0.	0.	0.	0.	0.	1.	0.	0.	0.	1.	0.	0.	0.	0.	0.	0.	0.	0.	0.	0.	0.
E 6	0.	1.	1.	1.	1.	1.	1.	1.	1.	1.	1.	0.	0.	0.	0.	0.	1.	0.	0.	0.	0.
CT-P&S	1.	1.	1.	1.	1.	1.	0.	0.	0.	0.	0.	0.	0.	0.	0.	0.	0.	0.	0.	0.	0.
CT-TECH	0.	0.	0.	0.	0.	0.	0.	0.	0.	0.	0.	0.	0.	0.	0.	0.	0.	0.	0.	0.	0.
Years Service	5.	5.	5.	5.	5.	5.	5.	5.	5.	5.	5.	5.	5.	5.	5.	5.	5.	5.	5.	5.	5.
Constant	1.	1.	1.	1.	1.	1.	1.	1.	1.	1.	1.	1.	1.	1.	1.	1.	1.	1.	1.	1.	1.

	22	23	24	25	26	27	28	29	30	31	32	33	34	35	36	37	38	39	40	41	42
Age	25.	35.	45.	25.	35.	45.	25.	35.	45.	25.	35.	45.	25.	35.	45.	25.	35.	45.	25.	35.	45.
E 1	0.	0.	0.	1.	1.	1.	0.	0.	0.	0.	0.	0.	0.	0.	0.	0.	0.	0.	0.	0.	0.
E 2	0.	0.	0.	0.	0.	0.	0.	0.	0.	0.	0.	1.	0.	0.	0.	0.	0.	0.	0.	0.	0.
E 4	0.	0.	0.	0.	0.	0.	0.	0.	0.	1.	0.	0.	0.	1.	0.	0.	0.	0.	0.	0.	0.
E 5	0.	0.	0.	0.	0.	0.	0.	0.	0.	0.	0.	0.	0.	0.	0.	0.	0.	0.	0.	0.	0.
E 6	0.	0.	0.	0.	0.	0.	0.	0.	1.	0.	0.	0.	0.	0.	0.	1.	1.	1.	0.	0.	0.
CT-P&S	1.	1.	1.	1.	1.	1.	1.	1.	1.	1.	1.	0.	0.	0.	0.	0.	0.	0.	0.	0.	0.
CT-TECH	0.	0.	0.	0.	0.	0.	0.	0.	0.	0.	0.	0.	0.	0.	0.	0.	0.	0.	0.	0.	0.
Years Service	5.	5.	5.	5.	5.	5.	5.	5.	5.	5.	5.	5.	5.	5.	5.	5.	5.	5.	5.	5.	5.
Constant	1.	1.	1.	1.	1.	1.	1.	1.	1.	1.	1.	1.	1.	1.	1.	1.	1.	1.	1.	1.	1.

	43	44	45	46	47	48	49	50	51	52	53	54	55	56	57	58	59	60	61	62	63
Age	35.	45.	35.	45.	35.	45.	35.	45.	35.	45.	35.	45.	35.	45.	35.	45.	35.	45.	35.	45.	35.
E 1	0.	0.	0.	0.	0.	0.	0.	0.	0.	0.	0.	0.	0.	0.	0.	0.	0.	0.	0.	0.	0.
E 2	0.	0.	0.	0.	0.	0.	0.	0.	0.	0.	0.	0.	0.	0.	0.	0.	0.	0.	0.	0.	0.
E 4	1.	0.	0.	0.	0.	0.	0.	0.	0.	0.	0.	0.	0.	0.	0.	0.	0.	0.	0.	0.	0.
E 5	0.	0.	0.	0.	0.	0.	0.	0.	0.	0.	0.	0.	0.	0.	0.	0.	0.	0.	0.	0.	0.
E 6	0.	0.	0.	0.	0.	0.	0.	0.	0.	0.	0.	0.	0.	0.	0.	0.	0.	0.	0.	0.	0.
CT-P&S	0.	0.	0.	0.	0.	0.	0.	0.	0.	0.	0.	0.	0.	0.	0.	0.	0.	0.	0.	0.	0.
CT-TECH	0.	0.	0.	0.	0.	0.	0.	0.	0.	0.	0.	0.	0.	0.	0.	0.	0.	0.	0.	0.	0.
Years Service	10.	10.	10.	10.	10.	10.	10.	10.	10.	10.	10.	10.	10.	10.	10.	10.	10.	10.	10.	10.	10.
Constant	1.	1.	1.	1.	1.	1.	1.	1.	1.	1.	1.	1.	1.	1.	1.	1.	1.	1.	1.	1.	1.

TABLE A7-1 (cont'd)

	64	65	66	67	68	69	70	71	72	73	74	75	76	77	78	79	80	81	82	83	84
Age	45.	35.	35.	35.	45.	35.	45.	35.	45.	45.	45.	35.	45.	35.	45.	35.	45.	35.	45.	35.	45.
E 1	0.	0.	0.	0.	0.	0.	0.	0.	0.	0.	0.	0.	0.	0.	0.	0.	0.	0.	0.	0.	0.
E 2	0.	0.	1.	1.	0.	1.	0.	1.	0.	0.	0.	1.	0.	1.	0.	1.	0.	1.	0.	1.	0.
E 4	1.	1.	0.	0.	1.	0.	1.	0.	1.	1.	1.	0.	1.	0.	1.	0.	1.	0.	1.	0.	1.
E 5	0.	0.	0.	0.	0.	0.	0.	0.	0.	0.	0.	0.	0.	0.	0.	0.	0.	0.	0.	0.	0.
E 6	0.	0.	0.	0.	1.	0.	0.	0.	1.	0.	1.	0.	1.	0.	1.	0.	1.	0.	1.	0.	1.
CT-P&S	0.	0.	0.	0.	0.	0.	0.	0.	0.	0.	0.	0.	0.	0.	0.	0.	0.	0.	0.	0.	0.
CT-TECH	0.	0.	0.	0.	0.	0.	0.	0.	0.	0.	0.	0.	0.	0.	0.	0.	0.	0.	0.	0.	0.
Years Service	10.	10.	10.	10.	10.	10.	10.	15.	15.	15.	15.	15.	15.	15.	15.	15.	15.	15.	15.	15.	15.
Constant	1.	1.	1.	1.	1.	1.	1.	1.	1.	1.	1.	1.	1.	1.	1.	1.	1.	1.	1.	1.	1.

	85	86	87	88	89	90	91	92	93	94	95	96	97	98
Age	35.	45.	35.	45.	45.	35.	35.	35.	45.	45.	45.	35.	45.	45.
E 1	0.	0.	1.	0.	1.	0.	0.	0.	0.	0.	0.	0.	0.	0.
E 2	0.	0.	0.	1.	0.	1.	0.	1.	0.	1.	0.	0.	0.	0.
E 4	0.	0.	0.	0.	0.	0.	0.	0.	0.	0.	0.	0.	0.	0.
E 5	0.	0.	0.	0.	0.	0.	0.	0.	0.	0.	0.	0.	0.	0.
E 6	1.	0.	0.	0.	0.	0.	1.	0.	0.	0.	0.	1.	0.	0.
CT-P&S	1.	0.	0.	0.	0.	0.	1.	0.	0.	0.	0.	0.	0.	0.
CT-TECH	1.	1.	1.	1.	1.	1.	1.	1.	1.	1.	1.	1.	1.	1.
Years Service	15.	15.	15.	15.	15.	15.	15.	15.	15.	15.	15.	15.	15.	15.
Constant	1.	1.	1.	1.	1.	1.	1.	1.	1.	1.	1.	1.	1.	1.

* "Zero" and "one" indicate, respectively, the absence or presence of a qualitative characteristic.

TABLE A7-2

Salary Projections by Ethnolinguistic Category, for All Possible Combinations

	1	2	3	4	5	6	7	8	9	10
All Francophones	$ 7,563.04	8,345.84	9,128.64	8,409.44	9,192.24	9,975.04	7,388.01	8,170.81	8,953.61	7,134.50
Unilingual French	8,167.79	8,661.69	9,155.59	7,642.94	8,136.84	8,630.74	7,587.06	8,080.96	8,574.86	6,373.96
Bilingual French	7,445.93	8,215.93	9,985.93	9,008.41	9,778.41	10,548.41	7,474.91	8,244.91	9,014.91	7,424.75
All Anglophones	6,694.58	8,192.68	9,690.78	8,667.62	10,165.72	11,663.82	7,532.97	9,031.07	10,529.17	7,664.51
Unilingual English	6,924.84	8,229.64	9,534.44	9,485.57	10,790.37	12,095.17	7,633.39	8,938.19	10,242.99	8,237.52
Bilingual English	5,540.85	8,059.75	10,578.65	6,651.29	9,170.19	11,689.09	6,275.40	8,794.30	11,313.20	5,483.43

	11	12	13	14	15	16	17	18	19	20
All Francophones	7,917.36	8,700.16	6,013.38	6,796.18	7,578.98	6,693.42	7,476.22	8,259.02	8,037.62	8,820.42
Unilingual French	6,567.86	7,361.76	6,700.20	7,194.10	7,688.00	6,698.32	7,192.22	7,686.12	8,566.76	9,060.66
Bilingual French	8,194.75	8,964.75	5,910.89	6,680.89	7,450.89	6,932.31	7,702.31	8,472.31	7,751.54	8,521.54
All Anglophones	9,162.61	10,660.71	4,691.33	6,189.43	7,687.53	5,614.74	7,112.84	8,610.94	6,532.48	8,030.58
Unilingual English	9,542.32	10,847.92	4,744.92	6,049.72	7,354.52	5,828.96	7,133.76	8,438.56	6,254.46	7,559.26
Bilingual English	8,002.33	10,521.23	4,201.20	6,720.10	9,239.00	4,758.18	7,277.08	9,795.98	7,528.79	10,047.69

	21	22	23	24	25	26	27	28	29	30
All Francophones	9,603.22	7,609.14	8,391.94	9,174.76	6,494.52	7,277.32	8,060.12	7,174.56	7,957.36	8,740.16
Unilingual French	9,554.56	6,772.93	7,266.83	7,760.73	5,888.95	6,382.85	6,076.75	5,887.07	6,380.97	6,874.87
Bilingual French	9,291.54	7,730.36	8,500.36	9,270.36	6,635.14	7,405.14	8,175.14	7,656.56	8,426.56	9,196.56
All Anglophones	9,528.68	7,502.41	9,000.51	10,498.61	5,285.49	6,783.59	8,281.69	6,208.90	7,707.00	9,205.10
Unilingual English	8,864.06	7,567.14	8,871.94	10,176.74	5,348.71	6,653.51	7,950.31	6,432.75	7,737.55	9,042.35
Bilingual English	12,566.59	7,471.37	9,990.27	12,509.17	4,035.41	6,554.31	9,073.21	4,592.39	7,111.29	9,630.19

	31	32	33	34	35	36	37	38	39	40
All Francophones	8,518.76	9,301.56	10,084.36	9,365.16	10,147.96	10,930.76	8,343.73	9,126.53	9,909.33	8,090.28
Unilingual French	7,755.51	8,249.41	8,743.31	7,230.66	7,724.56	8,218.46	7,174.78	7,668.68	8,162.58	5,961.68
Bilingual French	8,475.79	9,245.79	10,015.79	10,038.27	10,808.27	11,578.27	8,504.77	9,274.77	10,044.77	8,454.61
All Anglophones	7,126.64	8,624.74	10,122.84	9,099.68	10,597.78	12,095.88	7,965.03	9,463.13	10,761.23	8,096.57
Unilingual English	6,858.25	8,163.05	9,467.85	9,418.98	10,723.78	12,028.58	7,566.80	8,871.60	10,176.40	8,170.93
Bilingual English	7,363.00	9,881.90	12,400.80	8,473.44	10,992.34	13,511.24	8,097.55	10,616.45	13,135.35	7,305.58

TABLE A7-2 (cont'd)

	41	42	43	44	45	46	47	48	49	50
All Francophones	$ 8,873.08	$ 9,655.88	$ 8,363.89	$ 9,146.69	$ 9,210.29	$ 9,993.09	$ 8,188.86	$ 8,971.66	$ 7,935.41	$ 8,518.21
Unilingual French	6,455.58	6,949.68	8,817.39	9,311.29	8,292.54	8,786.44	8,236.66	8,730.56	7,023.56	7,517.46
Bilingual French	9,224.61	9,994.61	8,199.83	8,969.83	9,762.31	10,532.31	8,228.81	8,998.81	8,178.65	8,948.65
All Anglophones	9,594.67	11,092.77	8,365.43	9,063.53	10,338.47	11,836.57	9,203.82	10,701.92	9,335.36	10,833.46
Unilingual English	9,475.73	10,780.53	8,546.39	9,831.19	11,107.12	12,411.92	9,254.94	10,559.74	9,859.07	11,163.87
Bilingual English	9,824.48	12,343.38	7,680.35	10,199.25	8,790.79	11,309.69	8,414.90	10,933.80	7,622.93	10,141.83

	51	52	53	54	55	56	57	58	59	60
All Francophones	6,814.23	7,597.03	7,494.27	8,277.07	8,838.47	9,621.27	8,409.99	9,192.79	7,295.37	8,078.17
Unilingual French	7,349.80	7,843.70	7,347.92	7,841.82	9,216.36	9,710.26	7,422.53	7,916.43	6,558.55	7,032.45
Bilingual French	6,664.79	7,434.79	7,686.21	8,456.21	8,505.44	9,275.44	8,484.26	9,254.26	7,389.04	8,159.04
All Anglophones	6,362.18	7,860.28	7,285.59	8,783.69	8,203.33	9,701.26	9,173.26	10,671.36	6,956.34	8,454.44
Unilingual English	6,366.47	7,671.27	7,450.51	8,755.31	7,876.01	9,180.81	9,188.69	10,493.49	6,970.26	8,275.06
Bilingual English	6,340.70	8,859.60	6,897.68	9,416.58	9,668.29	12,187.19	9,610.87	12,129.77	6,174.91	8,693.81

	61	62	63	64	65	66	67	68	69	70
All Francophones	7,975.41	8,758.21	9,319.61	10,102.41	10,166.01	10,948.81	9,144.58	9,927.38	8,891.13	9,673.93
Unilingual French	6,536.67	7,030.57	8,405.11	8,899.01	7,880.26	8,374.16	7,824.28	8,318.28	6,611.28	7,105.18
Bilingual French	8,410.46	9,180.46	9,229.69	9,999.69	10,792.17	11,562.17	9,258.67	10,028.67	9,208.51	9,978.51
All Anglophones	7,879.75	9,377.85	8,797.49	10,295.59	10,770.53	12,268.63	9,635.88	11,133.98	9,767.42	11,265.52
Unilingual English	8,054.30	9,359.10	8,479.80	9,784.60	11,040.53	12,345.33	9,188.35	10,493.15	9,792.48	11,097.28
Bilingual English	6,731.89	9,250.79	9,502.50	12,021.40	10,612.94	13,131.84	10,237.05	12,755.95	9,445.08	11,963.98

	71	72	73	74	75	76	77	78	79	80
All Francophones	8,381.94	9,164.74	9,228.34	10,011.14	8,206.91	8,989.71	7,953.46	8,736.26	6,832.28	7,615.08
Unilingual French	8,973.09	9,466.99	8,448.24	8,942.14	8,392.36	8,886.26	7,179.26	7,673.16	7,505.50	7,999.40
Bilingual French	8,183.73	8,953.73	9,746.21	10,516.21	8,212.71	8,982.71	8,162.55	8,932.55	6,648.69	7,418.69
All Anglophones	8,538.18	10,036.28	10,511.22	12,009.32	9,376.57	10,874.67	9,508.11	11,006.21	6,534.93	8,033.03
Unilingual English	8,863.14	10,167.94	11,423.87	12,728.67	9,571.69	10,876.49	10,175.82	11,480.62	6,683.62	7,988.02
Bilingual English	7,300.95	9,819.85	8,411.39	10,930.29	8,035.50	10,554.40	7,243.53	9,762.43	5,961.30	8,480.20

TABLE A7-2 (end)

	81	82	83	84	85	86	87	88	89	90
All Francophones	$ 7,512.32	$ 8,295.12	$ 8,856.52	$ 9,639.32	$ 8,428.04	$ 9,210.84	$ 7,313.42	$ 8,096.22	$ 7,993.46	$ 8,776.26
Unilingual French	7,503.62	7,997.52	9,372.06	9,865.96	7,578.23	8,072.13	6,694.25	7,188.15	6,692.37	7,186.27
Bilingual French	7,670.11	8,440.11	8,489.34	9,259.34	8,468.16	9,238.16	7,372.94	8,142.94	8,394.36	9,164.36
All Anglophones	7,458.34	8,956.44	8,376.08	9,874.18	9,346.01	10,844.11	7,129.09	8,627.19	8,052.50	9,550.60
Unilingual English	7,767.26	9,072.06	8,192.76	9,497.56	9,505.44	10,810.24	7,287.01	8,591.81	8,371.05	9,675.85
Bilingual English	6,518.28	9,037.18	9,288.89	11,807.79	9,231.47	11,750.37	5,795.51	8,314.41	6,352.49	8,871.39

	91	92	93	94	95	96	97	98
All Francophones	9,337.66	10,120.46	10,184.06	10,966.86	9,162.63	9,945.63	8,909.18	9,691.98
Unilingual French	8,560.81	9,054.71	8,035.96	8,529.86	7,980.08	8,473.98	6,766.98	7,260.88
Bilingual French	9,213.59	9,983.59	10,776.07	11,546.07	9,242.57	10,012.57	9,192.41	9,962.41
All Anglophones	8,970.24	10,468.34	10,943.28	12,441.38	9,808.63	11,306.73	9,940.17	11,438.27
Unilingual English	8,796.55	10,101.35	11,357.28	12,662.08	9,505.10	10,809.90	10,109.23	11,414.03
Bilingual English	9,123.10	11,642.00	10,233.54	12,752.44	9,857.65	12,376.55	9,065.68	11,584.58

TABLE A/-3

Predicted Salary Differentials (Francophones Less Anglophones) For All Combinations

	1	2	3	4	5	6	7	8	9	10	11
All	$ 868.5	153.2	-562.1	-258.2	-973.5	-1,688.8	-145.0	-860.3	-1,575.6	-529.9	-1,245.2
Unilingual	1,243.0	432.1	-378.8	-1,842.6	-2,653.5	-3,464.4	-46.3	-857.2	-1,668.1	-1,863.6	-2,674.5
Bilingual	1,905.1	156.2	-1,592.7	2,357.1	608.2	-1,140.7	1,199.5	-549.4	-2,298.3	1,941.3	192.4

	12	13	14	15	16	17	18	19	20	21	22
All	-1,960.5	1,322.1	606.8	-108.5	1,078.7	363.4	-351.9	1,505.1	789.8	74.5	106.7
Unilingual	-3,485.4	1,955.3	1,144.4	333.5	869.4	58.5	-752.4	2,312.3	1,501.4	690.5	-794.2
Bilingual	-1,556.5	1,709.7	-39.2	-788.1	2,174.1	425.2	-1,323.7	222.8	-1,526.1	-3,275.0	259.0

	23	24	25	26	27	28	29	30	31	32	33
All	-608.6	-1,323.9	1,209.0	493.7	-221.6	965.7	250.4	-464.9	1,392.1	676.8	-38.5
Unilingual	-1,605.1	-2,416.0	540.2	-270.7	-1,081.6	-545.7	-1,356.6	-2,167.5	897.3	86.4	-724.5
Bilingual	-1,489.9	-3,238.8	2,599.7	850.8	-898.1	3,064.2	1,315.3	-433.6	1,112.8	-636.1	-2,385.0

	34	35	36	37	38	39	40	41	42	43	44
All	265.5	-449.8	-1,165.1	378.7	-336.6	-1,051.9	-6.3	-721.6	-1,436.9	-1.5	-716.8
Unilingual	-2,188.3	-2,999.2	-3,810.1	-392.0	-1,202.9	-2,013.8	-2,209.2	-3,020.2	-3,831.0	271.0	-539.9
Bilingual	1,564.8	-184.1	-1,933.0	407.2	-1,341.7	-3,090.6	1,149.0	-599.9	-2,348.8	519.5	-1,229.4

	45	46	47	48	49	50	51	52	53	54	55
All	-1,128.2	-1,843.5	-1,015.0	-1,730.3	-1,399.9	-2,115.2	452.1	-263.4	208.7	-506.6	635.1
Unilingual	-2,814.6	-3,625.5	-1,018.3	-1,829.2	-2,835.5	-3,646.4	983.3	172.4	-102.6	-913.5	1,340.4
Bilingual	971.5	-777.4	-186.1	-1,935.0	555.7	-1,193.2	324.1	-1,424.8	788.5	-960.4	-1,162.8

	56	57	58	59	60	61	62	63	64	65	66
All	-48.0	-1,478.6	-80.2	339.0	-376.3	95.7	-619.6	522.1	-193.2	-604.5	-1,319.8
Unilingual	-955.3	-2,577.1	529.5	-431.7	-1,242.6	1,517.6	-2,328.5	-74.7	-885.6	-3,160.3	-3,971.2
Bilingual	622.3	-2,875.5	-2,911.7	1,214.1	-534.8	1,678.6	-70.3	-272.8	-2,021.7	179.2	-1,569.7

TABLE A7-3 (cont'd)

	67	68	69	70	71	72	73	74	75	76	77
All	−491.3	−1,206.6	−876.3	−1,591.6	−156.2	−871.5	−1,262.9	−1,998.2	−1,169.7	−1,885.0	−1,554.9
Unilingual	−1,364.0	−2,174.9	−3,181.2	−3,992.1	110.0	−700.9	−2,975.6	−3,786.5	−1,179.3	−1,990.2	−2,996.4
Bilingual	−978.4	−2,727.3	−236.6	−1,985.5	882.8	−866.1	1,334.8	−414.1	177.2	−1,571.7	919.0

	78	79	80	81	82	83	84	85	86	87	88
All	−2,269.9	297.4	−417.9	54.0	−661.3	480.4	−234.9	−918.0	−1,633.3	184.3	−531.3
Unilingual	−3,807.5	822.3	11.4	−263.6	−1,074.5	1,179.3	368.4	−1,927.2	−2,738.1	−592.8	−1,403.5
Bilingual	−829.9	687.4	−1,016.5	1,151.8	−597.1	−799.5	−2,548.4	−763.3	−2,512.2	1,577.4	−171.8

	89	90	91	92	93	94	95	96	97	98
All	−59.0	−774.3	367.4	−347.9	−759.2	−1,474.5	−646.0	−1,361.3	−1,031.0	−1,746.3
Unilingual	−1,678.7	−2,489.6	−235.7	−1,046.6	−3,321.3	−4,132.2	−1,525.0	−2,335.9	−3,342.2	−4,153.1
Bilingual	2,041.9	293.0	90.5	−1,658.4	542.5	−1,206.4	−615.1	−2,364.0	126.7	−1,622.2

TABLE A7-4

Ratio of the Predicted Salary Differentials to Their Standard Errors

	1	2	3	4	5	6	7	8	9	10	11	12	13	14	15	16
All	.39	.07	.26	.12	.44	−.77	−.07	.39	−.72	−.24	.57	.89	.60	.28	.05	
Unilingual	.58	−.20	−.18	−.86	−1.25	−1.63	−.02	−.40	−.78	−.87	−1.26	−1.64	.92	.54	.16	
Bilingual	.35	.03	−.29	.43	.11	−.21	−.22	.10	−.42	.35	.04	−.28	.31	−.01	.33	

	17	18	19	20	21	22	23	24	25	26	27	28	29	30	31	32
All	.17	.16	.68	.36	.03	.05	.28	.60	.55	.22	.10	.44	.11	.21	.63	
Unilingual	.03	−.35	1.09	.70	.32	.37	.75	−.13	.25	.13	.51	.26	.64	−1.02	.42	
Bilingual	.08	−.24	.04	.28	−.60	−.05	−.27	.59	.47	.15	.16	.56	.24	−.08	.20	

	33	34	35	36	37	38	39	40	41	42	43	44	45	46	47	48
All	.33	.12	−.20	.53	.17	−.15	.48	−.00	.33	.65	−.00	.33	.51	.84	.46	
Unilingual	−.34	−1.03	−1.41	−1.79	.18	−.56	.95	−1.04	−1.42	−1.80	.13	.25	−1.32	−1.70	.48	
Bilingual	.43	.28	.03	.35	.07	−.24	.56	.21	.11	.43	.09	.22	.18	−.14	.03	

	49	50	51	52	53	54	55	56	57	58	59	60	61	62	63	64
All	.64	.96	.21	.12	.09	−.23	.29	.04	.35	.67	.15	.17	.04	.28	.24	
Unilingual	−1.33	−1.71	.46	.08	.05	−.43	.63	.25	−.83	−1.21	.20	.58	.71	−1.09	.04	
Bilingual	−.10	−.22	.06	.26	.14	.17	.21	.53	.21	.52	.22	.10	.31	.01	.05	

	65	66	67	68	69	70	71	72	73	74	75	76	77	78	79	80
All	−.27	−.60	.22	.55	−.40	−.72	.07	.40	.58	.91	.15	.86	.71	−1.03	.14	
Unilingual	−1.48	−1.86	.64	−1.02	−1.49	−1.87	.05	.33	−1.40	−1.78	.55	−.93	−1.41	−1.79	.39	
Bilingual	.03	−.29	.18	.50	−.04	.36	.16	.16	.24	−.08	.03	.29	.17	−.15	.13	

	81	82	83	84	85	86	87	88	89	90	91	92	93	94	95	96
All	.02	−.30	.22	.11	.42	−.74	.08	.24	.03	−.35	.17	.16	−.34	.67	.29	
Unilingual	−.12	−.50	.64	−1.02	−.90	−1.28	−.28	.66	.79	−1.17	.11	.49	−1.56	−1.94	−.72	
Bilingual	.21	−.11	.15	.46	.14	.46	.29	.03	.37	.05	.02	.30	.10	.22	.11	

	97	98
All	−.47	−.79
Unilingual	−1.57	−1.95
Bilingual	.02	.30

Bibliography

Ahmad, Muneer. *The Civil Servant in Pakistan*. (Karachi: Oxford University Press, 1964).

Alford, Robert R. *Party and Society, The Anglo-American Democracies*. (Chicago: Rand McNally and Co., 1963).

Anderson, Charles H. *White Protestant Americans: From National Origins to Religious Groups*. (Englewood Cliffs, New Jersey: Prentice-Hall, 1970).

Auclair, G.A. and W.H. Read. "A Cross-Cultural Study of Industrial Leadership." Research report prepared for Royal Commission on Bilingualism and Biculturalism, (Ottawa, 1966).

Banks, Arthur S. and Robert B. Textor. *A Cross-Polity Survey*. (Cambridge, Mass.: M.I.T. Press, 1965).

Beattie, Christopher, Jacques Désy and S. A. Longstaff. *Bureaucratic Careers: Anglophones and Francophones in the Canadian Public Service*. (Ottawa: Information Canada, 1972).

Beattie, Christopher and Byron G. Spencer, "Career Attainment in Canadian Bureaucracies: Unscrambling the Effects of Age, Seniority, Education, and Ethnolinguistic Factors on Salary," *American Journal of Sociology*. Vol. 77, No. 3 (November, 1971), 472-490.

Becker, Howard S. and Anselm L. Strauss, "Careers, Personality, and Adult Socialization." *American Journal of Sociology*, Vol. 62 (November, 1956), 253-263.

Bendix, Reinhard. *Higher Civil Servants in American Society. A Study of the Social Origins, the Careers, and the Power-Position of Higher Federal Administration*. (Boulder, Colorado: University of Colorado Press, 1949).

Bendix, Reinhard and Bennett Berger, "Images of Society and Problems of Concept Formation in Sociology." In Llewellyn Gross (ed.). *Symposium on Sociological Theory*. (Evanston, Ill.: Row, Peterson, and Co., 1959), 92-118.

Berger, Morroe. *Bureaucracy and Society in Modern Egypt. A Study of the Higher Civil Service*. (Princeton, N.J.: Princeton University Press, 1957).

Blalock, Hubert M., Jr. *Social Statistics*. (Toronto: McGraw-Hill, 1960).

Blalock, Hubert M., Jr. *Toward a Theory of Minority-Group Relations*. (New York: John Wiley and Sons, 1967).

Blau, Peter M. *The Dynamics of Bureaucracy, A Study of Inter-personal Relations in Two Government Agencies*. 2nd ed. (Chicago: University of Chicago Press, 1963).

Blauner, Robert. *Alienation and Freedom. The Factory Worker and His Industry*. (Chicago: The University of Chicago Press, 1964).

Borhek, J.T. "Ethnic-Group Cohesion," *American Journal of Sociology*, Vol. 76 (July, 1970), 33-46.

Brazeau, E. Jacques, "Language Differences and Occupational Experience," *Canadian Journal of Economics and Political Science*, Vol. 24 (November, 1958), 532-540.

Broom, Leonard and F. Lancaster Jones, "Career Mobility in Three Societies: Australia, Italy, and the United States," *American Sociological Review*, Vol. 34 (October, 1969), 650-658.

Canada Royal Commission on Bilingualism and Biculturalism. *The Work World*. Final Report, Vol. 3A. (Ottawa: Queen's Printer, 1969).

Canada (Government of). *Organization of the Government of Canada*. (Ottawa: The Queen's Printer, 1965).

Carlin, Jerome. *Lawyers on Their Own*. (New Brunswick, N.J.: Rutgers University Press, 1962).

Chapman, Brian. *The Profession of Government. The Public Service in Europe*. (London: Unwin University Books, 1959).

Clark, S.D. *Movements of Political Protest in Canada, 1640-1840*. (Toronto: University of Toronto Press, 1959).

Clark, S.D. *The Developing Canadian Community*. (Toronto: University of Toronto Press, 1962).

Clark, S.D. "Canada and Her Great Neighbour," *The Canadian Review of Sociology and Anthropology*, Vol. 1 (November, 1964), 193-201.

Comeau, Paul-André, "Acculturation ou assimilation: Technique d'analyse et tentative de mesure chez les franco-ontariens," *Canadian Journal of Political Science*, Vol. 2 (June, 1969), 158-172.

Cook, Ramsay. *Canada and the French-Canadian Question*. (Toronto: Macmillan of Canada, 1968).

Creighton, Donald G. *A History of Canada. Dominion of the North*. Revised and Enlarged Edition. (Boston: Houghton Mifflin, 1958).

Creighton, Donald G. *British North America at Confederation, A Study Prepared for the Royal Commission on Dominion-Provincial Relations, 1939*. (Ottawa: Queen's Printer, 1963).

Crozier, Michel. *The Bureaucratic Phenomenon*. (Chicago: University of Chicago Press, 1964).

Dahrendorf, Ralf, "Out of Utopia: Toward a Reorientation of Sociological Analysis," *American Journal of Sociology*, Vol. 64 (September, 1958). 115-127.

Dahrendorf, Ralf. *Society and Democracy in Germany*. (Garden City, N.Y.: Doubleday, 1967).

Dalton, Melville, "Informal Factors in Career Achievement," *American Journal of Sociology*, Vol. 56 (March, 1951), 407-415.

Demerath, N. J., III, and Richard A. Peterson (eds.). *System, Change and Conflict, A Reader on Contemporary Functional Theory and the Debate Over Functionalism*. (New York: The Free Press, 1967).

Diamond, Sigmund, "An Experiment in 'Feudalism': French Canada in the Seventeenth Century," *William and Mary Quarterly*, Vol. 18 (January, 1961), 3-34.

Diamond, Sigmund, "From Organization to Society: Virginia in the Seventeenth Century," *American Journal of Sociology*, Vol. 63 (March, 1958), 457-475.

Dofny, Jacques and Marcel Rioux, "Social Class in French Canada." In Marcel Rioux and Yves Martin (eds.), *French Canadian Society, Sociological Studies*, Vol. 1. The Carleton Library, (Toronto: McClelland and Stewart, 1964), 307-318. Originally published in French in 1962.

Duncan, Beverly and Otis Dudley Duncan, ''Minorities and the Process of Stratification,'' *American Sociological Review*, Vol. 33 (June, 1968), 356-364.

Durkheim, Emile. *The Division of Labor in Society*. Translated by George Simpson. (New York: The Free Press of Glencoe, 1964). First published in English, 1933; originally published in French, 1893.

Easterbrook, W. T. and Hugh G. J. Aitken. *Canadian Economic History*. (Toronto: The Macmillan Company, 1956).

Elkin, Frederick, ''Advertising Themes and Quiet Revolutions: Dilemmas in French Canada,'' *American Journal of Sociology*, Vol. 75 (July, 1969), 112-122.

Fishman, Joshua A., ''Some Contrasts Between Linguistically Homogeneous and Linguistically Heterogeneous Polities,'' *Sociological Inquiry*, Vol. 36 (Spring 1966), 146-158.

Forsey, Eugene, ''Parliament is Endangered by Mr. King's Principle.'' *Saturday Night*, October 9, 1949, 10-11.

Friedlander, Frank, ''Comparative Work Value Systems,'' *Personnel Psychology*, Vol. 18 (Spring 1965), 1-20.

Friedlander, Frank and Eugene Walton, ''Positive and Negative Motivations Toward Work,'' *Administrative Science Quarterly*, Vol. 9 (September, 1964), 194-207.

Gardner, R. C., E. Joy Wonnacott, and D. M. Taylor, ''Ethnic Stereotypes: A Factor Analytic Investigation,'' *Canadian Journal of Psychology*, Vol. 22 (August, 1968), 35-44.

Gordon, Milton M. *Assimilation in American Life, The Role of Race, Religion, and National Origins*. (New York: Oxford University Press, 1964).

Gouldner, Alvin W., ''Cosmopolitans and Locals: Toward an Analysis of Latent Social Roles—I, II,'' *Administrative Science Quarterly*, Vol. 2 (1957-58), 281-306, 444-480.

Guindon, Hubert, ''The Social Evolution of Quebec Reconsidered,'' *The Canadian Journal of Economics and Political Science*, Vol. 26 (November, 1960), 533-551.

Guindon, Hubert, ''Social Unrest, Social Class and Quebec's

Bureaucratic Revolution," *Queen's Quarterly*, Vol. 71 (Summer 1964), 150-162.

Hackett, Bruce M. *Higher Civil Servants in California, A Social and Political Portrait*. (Berkeley, Calif.: Institute of Governmental Studies, 1967).

Hall, Oswald, "The Informal Organization of the Medical Profession." *Canadian Journal of Economics and Political Science*, Vol. 12 (February, 1946), 30-44.

Hall, Richard H., "The Concept of Bureaucracy: An Empirical Assessment," *American Journal of Sociology*, Vol. 69 (July, 1963), 32-40.

Hall, Richard H. and Charles R. Tittle, "A Note on Bureaucracy and Its 'Correlates'," *American Journal of Sociology*, Vol. 72 (November, 1966), 267-272.

Heady, Ferrel. *Public Administration: A Comparative Perspective*. (Englewood Cliffs, N.J.: Prentice-Hall, 1966).

Herberg, Will. *Protestant-Catholic-Jew*. (New York: Doubleday and Co., 1955).

Herzberg, Frederick, *et. al. Job Attitudes: Review of Research and Opinion*. (Pittsburgh: Psychological Services of Pittsburgh, 1957).

Herzberg, Frederick, B. Mausner and Barbara Snyderman. *The Motivation to Work*. (New York: John Wiley and Sons, 1959).

Hodgetts, J. E. *The Canadian Public Service, A Physiology of Government, 1867-1970*. (Toronto: University of Toronto Press, 1973).

Hodgetts, J. E., "The Liberal and the Bureaucrat," *Queen's Quarterly*, Vol. 62 (Summer 1955), 176-183.

Hodgetts, J. E. *Pioneer Public Service: An Administrative History of the United Canadas, 1841-1867*. (Toronto: University of Toronto Press, 1955).

Hodgetts, J. E. *et. al. The Biography of an Institution: The Civil Service Commission of Canada, 1908-1967*. (Montreal: McGill-Queens Press, 1972).

Hughes, Everett C. *French Canada in Transition*. (Chicago: University of Chicago Press, 1943).

Hughes, Everett C., "Queries Concerning Industry and Society

Growing Out of Study of Ethnic Relations in Industry,'' *American Sociological Review*, Vol. 14 (April, 1949), 211-220.

Hutchinson, Edward Price. *Immigrants and Their Children, 1850-1950*. (New York: Wiley, 1956).

Inglehart, Ronald F. and Margaret Woodward, ''Language Conflicts and Political Community,'' *Comparative Studies in Society and History*, Vol. 10 (October, 1967), 27-45.

Johnstone, John W. C. *Young People's Images of Canadian Society, An Opinion Survey of Canadian Youth 13 to 20 Years of Age*. (Ottawa: Royal Commission on Bilingualism and Biculturalism, Internal Research Report, 1966).

Johnstone, John W. C. *et al*. *A Survey of the Canadian Public Service*. (Ottawa: Royal Commission on Bilingualism and Biculturalism Internal Research Report, 1966).

Kaplan, Abraham, ''Power in Perspective.'' In Robert L. Kahn and Elise Boulding (eds.), *Power and Conflict in Organizations*. (New York: Basic Books, 1964).

Kelsall, R.K. *Higher Civil Servants In Britain*. (London: Routledge and Kegan Paul, 1955).

Kelsall, R.K., ''The Social Background of the Higher Civil Service.'' In William A. Robson (ed.), *The Civil Service in Britain and France*. (London: The Hogarth Press, 1956), 151-160.

Kennedy, Ruby Jo Reeves, ''Single or Triple Melting Pot? Intermarriage Trends in New Haven, 1870-1940,'' *American Journal of Sociology*, Vol. 49 (January, 1944), 331-339.

Kennedy, Ruby Jo Reeves, ''Single or Triple Melting Pot? Intermarriage Trends in New Haven, 1870-1950,'' *American Journal of Sociology*, Vol. 58 (July, 1952), 56-59.

Keyfitz, Nathan, ''Canadians and Canadiens,'' *Queen's Quarterly*, Vol. 70 (Winter 1963), 163-182.

Keyfitz, Nathan, ''Foreward.'' In Everett C. Hughes, *French Canada in Transition*. (Chicago: The University of Chicago Press, 1963).

King, A. J. C. and Carol E. Angi. *Language and Secondary School Success*. (Ottawa: The Royal Commission on

Bilingualism and Biculturalism, Internal Research Report, 1966).

Kubota, Akira. *Higher Civil Servants in Postwar Japan*. (Princeton, N.J.: Princeton University Press, 1969).

Ladinsky, Jack, "Careers of Lawyers, Law Practice, and Legal Institutions," *American Sociological Review*, Vol. 28 (February, 1963), 47-54.

Lalande, Gilles. *The Department of External Affairs and Biculturalism*. (Ottawa: Queen's Printer, 1969).

Lanphier, C.M. and R.N. Morris, "Structural Aspects of Differences in Income between Anglophones and Francophones," *The Canadian Review of Sociology and Anthropology,* Vol. 11 (Feb., 1974), 53-66.

Lenski, Gerhard. *The Religious Factor*. Revised Edition. (Garden City, N.Y.: Doubleday, Anchor Books, 1963).

Lieberson, Stanley. *Ethnic Patterns in American Cities*. (New York: Free Press of Glencoe, 1963).

Lieberson, Stanley, "The Old-New Distinction and Immigrants in Australia," *American Sociological Review*, Vol. 28 (August, 1963), 550-565.

Lipset, Seymour Martin, "Canada and the United States: A Comparative View," *The Canadian Review of Sociology and Anthropology*, Vol. 1 (November, 1964), 173-185.

Lipset, Seymour Martin. *The First New Nation, The United States in Historical and Comparative Perspective*. (New York: Doubleday and Co., 1963).

Lipset, Seymour Martin, Martin A. Trow, James S. Coleman. *Union Democracy: The Internal Politics of the International Typographical Union*. (Glencoe, Ill.: The Free Press, 1956).

Lorwin, Val. R., "Belgium: Religion, Class, and Language in National Politics." In Robert A. Dahl (ed.), *Political Oppositions in Western Democracies*. (New Haven: Yale University Press, 1966), 147-87.

Lower, Arthur R. M. *Colony To Nation, A History of Canada*. 4th ed. (Don Mills, Ontario: Longmans Canada, 1964).

Marsh, Robert M. *Comparative Sociology: A Codification of Cross-Societal Analysis*. (New York: Harcourt, Brace and World, 1967).

Marvick, Dwaine. *Career Perspectives in a Bureaucratic Setting*. (Ann Arbor: University of Michigan Press, 1954).

Mayer, Kurt B., "Social Stratification in Two Equalitarian Societies: Australia and the United States," *Social Research*, Vol. 31 (Winter 1964), 435-465.

Meisel, John, "The Formulation of Liberal and Conservative Programmes in the 1957 Canadian General Election," *Canadian Journal of Economics and Political Science*, Vol. 26 (November, 1960), 565-574.

Melichar, Emanuel, "Least Squares Analysis of Economic Survey Data," *American Statistical Association, Proceedings of the Business and Economic Statistics Section*, 1965, 373-385.

Merton, Robert K., "Bureaucratic Structure and Personality." In Robert K. Merton, *Social Theory and Social Structure*. (Glencoe, Ill.: The Free Press, 1957), 195-206.

Migué, Jean-Luc, "Le nationalisme, l'unité nationale et la théorie économique de l'information," *Canadian Journal of Economics*, Vol. 3 (May, 1970), 183-198.

Naegele, Kaspar D., "Canadian Society: Some Reflections." In Bernard R. Blishen, *et. al*. (eds.), *Canadian Society, Sociological Perspectives*. (Toronto: The Macmillan Co. of Canada, 1961), 1-53.

Newman, Peter C., "The Ottawa Establishment," *Maclean's*, August 22, 1964.

Peabody, Robert A. and Francis E. Rourke, "Public Bureaucracies." In James G. March (ed.). *Handbook of Organizations*. (Chicago: Rand McNally, 1965), 802-837.

Peat, Marwick, Mitchell, and Co. *The Proposed Organization, Department of Public Works*. (July, 1965).

Perrow, Charles, "A Framework For The Comparative Analysis of Organizations," *American Sociological Review*, Vol. 32 (April, 1967), 194-208.

Porter, John, "Higher Public Servants and the Bureaucratic Elite in Canada," *Canadian Journal of Economics and Political Science*, Vol. 24 (November, 1958), 483-501.

Porter, John. *The Vertical Mosaic: An Analysis of Social Class and Power in Canada*. (Toronto: University of Toronto Press, 1965).

Porter, Lyman W. "Job Attitudes in Management: I. Perceived

Deficiences in Need Fulfillment as a Function of Job Level," *Journal of Applied Psychology,* Vol. 46 (December, 1962), 375-384.

Price, Charles. "Southern Europeans in Australia: Problems of Assimilation," *International Migration Review,* Vol. 2 (Summer 1968), 3-26.

Prives, M. Z. "Career and Promotion in the Federal Civil Service of Canada," *Canadian Public Administration,* Vol. 3 (1960), 179-190.

Quebec (Province). *Report of the Royal Commission of Inquiry on Constitutional Problems,* Vol. 3, Book 1. (Quebec City: Government of Quebec, 1956).

Quebec (Province). *Report of Royal Commission of Inquiry on Education in the Province of Quebec.* (Quebec City: Government of the Province of Quebec, 1963).

Quinn, Herbert F. *The Union Nationale. A Study in Quebec Nationalism.* (Toronto: University of Toronto Press, 1963).

Raynauld, André. *The Canadian Economic System.* (Toronto: The Macmillan Co. of Canada, 1967).

Richardson, Stephen A., "Organizational Contrasts on British and American Ships," *Administrative Science Quarterly,* Vol. 1 (September, 1956), 189-207.

Robson, William A. (ed.). *The Civil Service in Britain and France.* (New York: Macmillan, 1956).

Rocher, Guy, "Research on Occupations and Social Stratification." In Marcel Rioux and Yves Martin (eds.), *French-Canadian Society.* Vol. I. The Carleton Library, No. 18 (Toronto: McClelland and Stewart, 1964), 328-341.

Rosen, Bernard C., "Race, Ethnicity, and the Achievement Syndrome," *American Sociological Review,* Vol. 24 (February, 1959), 47-60.

Rosencrance, Richard N., "The Radical Culture of Australia." In Louis Hartz, *The Founding of New Societies.* (New York: Harcourt, Brace, and World, 1964), 275-318.

Russett, Bruce M. *et. al. World Handbook of Political and Social Indicators.* (New Haven, Connecticut: Yale University Press, 1964).

Scarrow, H. A. *The Higher Public Service of the Common-*

wealth of Australia. (Durham, N.C.: Duke University Press, 1957).

Schermerhorn, R. A. *Comparative Ethnic Relations*. (New York: Random House, 1970).

Smigel, Erwin O. *The Wall Street Lawyer*. (New York: The Free Press of Glencoe, 1964).

Social Research Group. *A Study of Inter-Ethnic Relations in Canada*. (Ottawa: Royal Commission on Bilingualism and Biculturalism, Internal Research Report), 1965.

Somers, Robert H., "A New Asymmetric Measure of Association for Ordinal Variables," *American Sociological Review*, Vol. 27 (December, 1962), 799-811.

Stanley, David T. *The Higher Civil Service; An Evaluation of Federal Personnel Practices*. (Washington: Brookings Institution, 1964).

Sterns, Dr. A. A. *History of the Department of Finance*. (Ottawa: Published Privately, May, 1965).

Stinchcombe, Arthur, "Bureaucratic and Craft Administration of Production: A Comparative Study," *Administrative Science Quarterly*, Vol. 4 (September, 1959), 168-187.

Subramaniam, V., "Representative Bureaucracy: A Reassessment," *American Political Science Review*, Vol. 61 (December, 1967), 1010-1019.

Suits, Daniel B., "Use of Dummy Variables in Regression Equations," *Journal of the American Statistical Association*, Vol. 52 (December, 1957), 548-551.

Taft, Ronald. *From Stranger to Citizen, A Survey of Studies of Immigrant Assimilation in Western Australia*, (London: Tavistock Publications, 1966).

Taylor, Herbert. *The Output of Canadian Universities and Colleges, 1962-65*. (Ottawa: The Royal Commission on Bilingualism and Biculturalism, Internal Research Report, 1966).

Taylor, Norman W., "The Effects of Industrialization: Its Opportunities and Consequences upon French-Canadian Society," *Journal of Economic History*, Vol. 20 (December), 1960, 638-47.

Taylor, Norman W., "The French Canadian Industrial Entrepreneur and His Social Environment." In Marcel Rioux and Yves Martin (eds.), *French-Canadian Society*. Vol. 1. (Toronto: McClelland and Stewart, 1964).

Trudeau, Pierre Elliott, "Some Obstacles to Democracy in Quebec," *Canadian Journal of Economics and Political Science*, Vol. 24 (August, 1958), 297-311.

Turner, Ralph H., "Sponsored and Contest Mobility and the School System," *American Sociological Review*, Vol. 25 (December, 1960), 855-867.

Udy, Stanley H., Jr., " 'Bureaucracy' and 'Rationality' in Weber's Organization Theory: An Empirical Study," *American Sociological Review*, Vol. 24 (December, 1959), 791-795.

Udy, Stanley H., Jr., "The Comparative Analysis of Organizations." In James G. March, (ed.), *Handbook of Organizations*. (Chicago: Rand McNally and Company, 1965), 678-709.

Vallier, Ivan, "Empirical Comparisons of Social Structure: Leads and Lags." In Ivan Vallier (ed.). *Comparative Methods in Sociology: Essays on Trends and Applications.* (Berkeley, Calif.: University of California Press, 1971).

Van Loon, Richard J. and Michael S. Whittington. *The Canadian Political System: Environment, Structure and Process*. (Toronto: McGraw-Hill Co., 1971).

Van Riper, Paul P. *History of the United States Civil Service*. (Evanston, Ill.: Row, Peterson and Co., 1958).

Wade, Mason. *The French Canadians, 1760-1967*. Revised Edition in Two Volumes. (Toronto: Macmillan of Canada, 1968).

Warner, W. Lloyd and Leo Srole. *The Social Systems of American Ethnic Groups*. (New Haven: Yale University Press, 1945).

Warner, W. Lloyd, *et. al. The American Fed* (New Haven: Yale University Press, 19

Weber, Max. *From Max Weber: Essays in S* lated, Edited, and with an Introduction b C. Wright Mills (New York: Oxford 1947).

Weber, Max. *The Theory of Socia*

Organization. Translated by A. M. Henderson and Talcott Parsons. Edited with an Introduction by Talcott Parsons. (London: William Hodge and Co., 1947).

Wilensky, Harold L. *Intellectuals in Labor Unions: Organizational Pressures on Professional Roles*. (Glencoe, Ill.: The Free Press, 1956).

Wilensky, Harold L., "Measures and Effects of Social Mobility." In Neil J. Smelser and Seymour Martin Lipset (eds.), *Social Structure and Mobility in Economic Development*. (Chicago: Aldine Publishing Company, 1966), 98-140.

Wilensky, Harold L., "Orderly Careers and Social Participation: The Impact of Work History on Social Integration in the Middle Mass," *American Sociological Review*, Vol. 26 (August, 1961), 521-539.

Wilensky, Harold L., "Work, Careers, and Social Integration," *International Social Science Journal*, Vol. 12 (Fall, 1960), 543-560.

Wilensky, Harold L. and Jack Ladinsky, "From Religious Community to Occupational Group: Structural Assimilation Among Professors, Lawyers, and Engineers," *American Sociological Review*, Vol. 32 (August, 1967), 541-561.

Williams, Robin M., Jr. *American Society. A Sociological Interpretation*. 2nd ed., Revised. (New York: Alfred A. Knopf, 1961).

Wrong, Dennis, "The Oversocialized Conception of Man in Modern Sociology," *American Sociological Review*, Vol. 26 (April, 1961), 183-193.

Zubrzycki, Jerzy. *Immigrants in Australia, A Demographic Survey Based Upon the 1954 Census.* (Melbourne: Melbourne University Press, 1960).

Zubrzycki, Jerzy, "Some Aspects of Structural Assimilation of Immigrants in Australia," *International Migration,* Vol. 6 (1968), 102-110.

Subject Index to Major Concepts and Topics

(Note: Page numbers in bold face type refer to definitions and major discussions.)

THE CARLETON LIBRARY